DATE DUE

JUN 14 1978

JUL 5 1978   JAN 1 8 1979
AU
A

'AU
SEP

OCT

OCT

O
C

DEC
DE
FE

FE

AP

W9-ASI-576

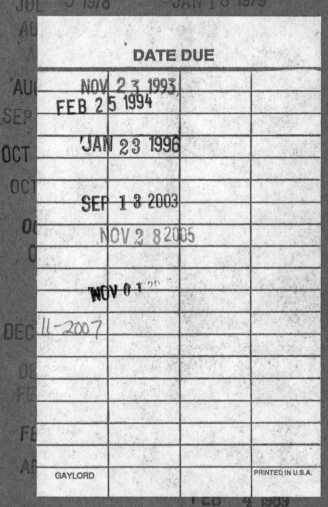

DATE DUE

NOV 2 3 1993			
FEB 2 5 1994			
'JAN 2 3 1996			
SEP 1 3 2003			
NOV 2 8 2005			
NOV 0 1 20			
ll-2007			
GAYLORD		PRINTED IN U.S.A.

FEB 4 1989

AND I ALONE SURVIVED

Copyright © 1978 by Lauren Elder and Shirley Streshinsky
All rights reserved. Printed in the U.S.A.

A Rose & Asseyev Project

No part of this publication may be reproduced or transmitted in any form or by any means, electronic or mechanical, including photocopy, recording or any information storage and retrieval system now known or to be invented, without permission in writing from the publisher, except by a reviewer who wishes to quote brief passages in connection with a review written for inclusion in a magazine, newspaper or broadcast.

For information contact: E. P. Dutton, 2 Park Avenue, New York, N.Y. 10016

LIBRARY OF CONGRESS CATALOGING IN PUBLICATION DATA

Elder, Lauren.
  And I Alone Survived
  "Thomas Congdon books."
  1. Survival (after airplane accidents, shipwrecks, etc.)   2. Aeronautics—California—Accidents—1976.
I. Streshinsky, Shirley, Joint author.   II. Title.
TL553.7.E43   979.4′794′86050924 [B]   77-20208

0-525-05481-2

Published simultaneously in Canada by Clarke, Irwin & Company Limited, Toronto and Vancouver
    10 9 8 7 6 5 4 3 2

AND I ALONE SURVIVED

Lauren Elder

with Shirley Streshinsky

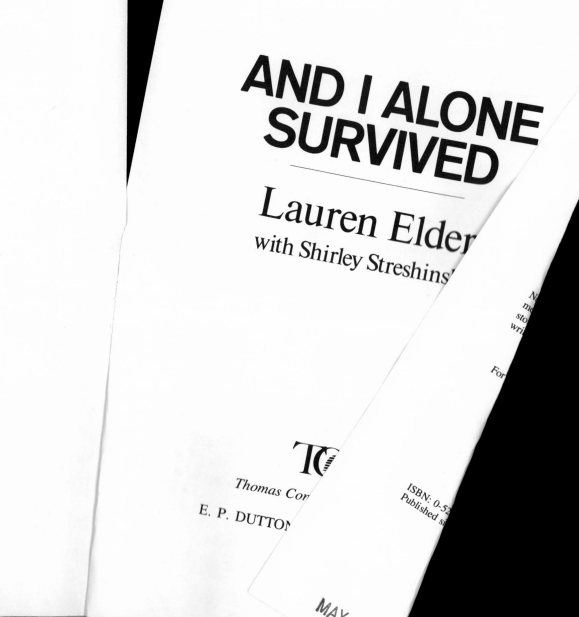

Thomas Cor

E. P. DUTTON

ISBN: 0-52
Published si

MAY

For my mother and father

And I only am escaped alone to tell thee. —*Job*

AND I ALONE SURVIVED

Lauren Elder
with Shirley Streshinsky

979.479
ELD

Thomas Congdon Books

E. P. DUTTON | NEW YORK

Glenview Public Library
1930 Glenview Road
Glenview, Illinois

Copyright © 1978 by Lauren Elder and Shirley Streshinsky
All rights reserved. Printed in the U.S.A.

A Rose & Asseyev Project

No part of this publication may be reproduced or transmitted in any form or by any means, electronic or mechanical, including photocopy, recording or any information storage and retrieval system now known or to be invented, without permission in writing from the publisher, except by a reviewer who wishes to quote brief passages in connection with a review written for inclusion in a magazine, newspaper or broadcast.

For information contact: E. P. Dutton, 2 Park Avenue, New York, N.Y. 10016

LIBRARY OF CONGRESS CATALOGING IN PUBLICATION DATA

Elder, Lauren.
  And I Alone Survived

  "Thomas Congdon books."
    1. Survival (after airplane accidents, shipwrecks,
etc.) 2. Aeronautics—California—Accidents—1976.
I. Streshinsky, Shirley, Joint author. II. Title.
TL553.7.E43   979.4′794′86050924 [B]   77-20208

ISBN: 0-525-05481-2
Published simultaneously in Canada by Clarke, Irwin & Company Limited, Toronto
and Vancouver
10 9 8 7 6 5 4 3 2

MAY 8 1978

AND I ALONE
SURVIVED

Acknowledgments

The authors would like to thank: Tamara Asseyev and Alex Rose, Miles Becker, Carlos Castenada for the teachings of Don Juan, Betty Anne Clarke, Bruce Feldmann, Jim Fizdale, Edna Gaghen, Peter Lee, Harry O'Connor, Richard Parks, Deborah Prigoff, Ted Streshinsky, the good people of Independence and Lone Pine who were there when it counted, and, especially, Tom Congdon.

Prologue

I make lists. I make them when the whole of a thing seems
beyond my grasp, when it seems as if I can understand only
through the sum of the parts. I make them after the fact,
when I need to find out what happened and what it means. If
it is possible to find out what it means.

One of my lists is bits of knowledge, disconnected pieces
of information I have gathered about a certain place, things I
know now that I did not know then.

For example, I know: that latitude *36 degrees 43 minutes
24 seconds* and longitude *118 degrees 20 minutes 18 seconds*
marks a point half a mile south of Mt. Bradley, just fifteen
feet short of the crest of the Sierra Nevada Mountains in California—John Muir's "Range of Light." The altitude at that
precise point is 12,360 feet, and the air when you pull it into
your lungs is thin and sharp and cold, achingly cold.

I know: that this section of the Sierra Nevada is called the

Whitney Quadrangle, named for the highest mountain in the country outside of Alaska. In a space only thirteen miles wide and seventeen miles long so many peaks tower above 13,000 feet that it is hard to single out Mt. Whitney; but it is there, to the south of Mt. Bradley, in the highest section of the hard, cold spine of the High Sierra.

The Whitney Quadrangle is a wilderness profound, high, and deep. It lies within Kings Canyon and Sequoia national parks and the Inyo National Forest, which means that it has been declared a wilderness forever. It is, in fact, not much changed since the Spaniard Fray Pedro Font first saw it 200 years ago and named it *una gran sierra nevada*—a great snowy range.

I did not know any of that before, and it is probably a good thing that I did not.

Neither did I realize just how long winter lasts at altitudes above 10,000 feet. Mark Twain knew the mountains of the Sierra Nevada. He once wrote, "There are only two seasons in the region . . . the breaking up of one winter and the beginning of the next."

I know: that on a bright day late in April, when the rest of the state is bathed in spring sunlight, the temperature on the Sierra crest can be ten degrees, though it seems warmer because the ultraviolet screen is not as effective at that elevation.

Then, when the sun begins to drop into the west, into the Pacific, it takes on a shade of lavender that is brilliant, luminescent. People who know the mountains have a name for that color: alpenglow. But as soon as the black closes in on the mountaintop and the color is gone, the temperature can plummet to well below zero.

Cold enough to freeze beer.

Cold enough to freeze blood.

Nothing can live, for long, exposed to the hard-blowing cold on the crest of the High Sierra.

I know that now.

I know too that on the eastern edge the mountains plunge in an almost vertical drop to the desert valley below. It is more than a mile of precipitous granite glinting in the cold light, a sight like nothing imagined—surging, powerful, awesome.

The name of the valley is Owens. Few people, even in California, know where it is. I have lived in the state, on and off, for most of my life, and I saw the valley for the first time only three years ago. It is an isolated place dotted by towns with names like Independence and Lone Pine, towns strung out on the two-lane blacktop that shoots dead center down the narrow valley floor, towns bordered by Paiute reservations. It is empty country.

There are a few people on the outside who have reason to know Owens Valley—among them, the Japanese-Americans who spent the war years in the concentration camp called Manzanar. I have only lately been to Manzanar. There is not much left of it: a guardhouse, a plaque, some concrete foundations marked with a year, 1942. It would have been cold there at the base of the mountains that wartime winter. I had not yet been born in 1942. That year my father was in the South Pacific, a fighter pilot, much-decorated.

Venturi action. That is something my father would have known about, but I did not. It is a term used by pilots to describe what happens when air is forced up and over the crest of a mountain. The air gains speed as it flows over the top, and then it tumbles down the other side of the mountain in a rotary action that is turbulent and dangerous. Small planes should fly well above air like that. But in high altitudes the air is thin and the wings of a plane do not have as much lift, as they do at sea level.

Something else: I notice things now that I would not have noticed before, like a small item on the fifth page of the morning newspaper, a wire-service report on six Greek mountain climbers killed in an avalanche on 9,334-foot Mt. Olympus. Four men and two women dead on Mt. Olympus.

I am startled at how regularly such accounts appear. Only this morning the San Francisco *Chronicle* reported on a young couple caught in a blizzard as they attempted to cross the Sierra crest at Paiute Pass. "She tried to get him to put his hands in his pockets," the paper says. "He refused." He froze to death; she was picked up by a helicopter and taken to a hospital in Owens Valley. Her feet were frozen.

In the tiny Trinity Episcopal Chapel in Lone Pine I am drawn to a stained-glass window dedicated to the memory of those town children who died on Mt. Williamson—children on their way to summer camp, flying out of this lonely valley with suitcases packed with new underwear and swimsuits, when the small plane that carried them slammed into the second-highest peak in the Whitney Quadrangle. I think, sometimes, of their parents. I wonder if they stand on the floor of Owens Valley, look up at the escarpment of the Sierras, and feel its sweep, its power, its violent beauty. I wonder if they try to separate Mt. Williamson from the dozens of peaks surrounding it, the way I try to single out Mt. Bradley. As if it is somehow important to know the exact spot, the place where it happened.

Fata morgana is the name given to the mirages that wanderers in the desert sometimes see. I have learned how it happens. The image of mountains is refracted in the hot layers of air hovering above the desert, so it appears as a reflection which thirsty travelers interpret as an oasis. It is an optical illusion; it can be photographed. The name comes from the legend of King Arthur, from a woman named Morgan le Fay, who is said to have used the mirages for her own purposes. Fata morgana combines elements of science, fantasy, and survival.

I know all of these things now. I did not know them then—"then" being the twenty-nine years of my life that came before 1976.

The First Day

I'd been indoors for ten days, recovering from a bad case of dysentery I'd caught in Mexico. In the air I might be able to gain a new perspective. I could pack my Nikon and take some photos from the plane. It would be wonderful just to be able to concentrate on form and color and design, even though I knew I should be doing something to earn money.

I walked over to the counter where my latest painting was propped and looked at it hard. It was a large piece, thirty by forty inches, executed in layers of water color wash that had been sanded, then worked in color pencil and pastel. My eyes wandered to a small cactus I had included in that painting. It was the kind that has big round pads. If you looked hard enough, you could see that it was also Mickey Mouse. I did that sometimes—put in bizarre, cartoonish, goofy kinds of transformed images.

I could feel the ideas begin to seep in and I stopped them short. If I went back to the painting I would feel guilty, knowing that I should be doing something to earn money. I should go over to the university and get after them to pay me for the job I'd done before we left on the trip. The thought of that job—all the miserable hours of drudgery putting together a catalogue, all the hours of proofreading statistical tables—made my stomach churn. But if I did that, or worked on a business card I had promised to design, or started any of the things that would bring in some cash, it would only make me want to be painting. That was the dilemma that had to be resolved. Somehow.

"Call him." This time my voice rang out. "Tell Jay I want to go."

The dilemma would wait. I remember thinking that morning that big decisions are often easier to put off than little ones, that I could move through a lifetime making little decisions and never quite get to the big ones. I picked up a marking pen and scrawled in big print across a sheet of paper: *I want to make a bold gesture with my life.*

But first I was going to buzz over to Death Valley for the

5

day, just climb into a nice little airplane and go whizzing over the mountains and be home again in time for supper. At that moment it seemed exactly the right thing to be doing on a fine spring morning.

Jim immediately shifted into high gear. In what seemed like one long motion he rinsed his tea cup and the espresso machine, dried his hands, picked up the phone, dialed, and spoke in the staccato shorthand he used with his friend.

"Jay? Jim. Listen, Lauren wants to go. Okay?"

There was a short pause and I thought: *Maybe he'll say no, and then I'll know I should stay here and do some thinking.* Half of me hoped he *would* say no.

Then Jim said, "Great, I'll tell her," and I knew Jay had agreed. Jim turned to me without smiling, which meant his thoughts were running several minutes ahead, probably to the work waiting for him at the veterinary clinic.

"It's all set. Jay said he'll call you in a little while with the details." As he was about to leave, Jim swooped to kiss me. Abraham, our parakeet, swooped at the same time and the two almost collided. We laughed. "Have fun," he said, squeezing out the door so the bird couldn't escape. "See you around six, I guess."

"I guess," I answered. I had no idea how long it took to fly to Death Valley and back. I had gone there three years earlier as a chaperone for a high school field trip; it had taken us twelve hours to drive back to the Bay Area, but I didn't know how to translate that into air hours.

After Jim went out the front door, I sat down, quiet and listening, alone in the big studio. Only the chirping of the birds and the fluttering of their wings filled the silence. I remembered that I had wanted to ask Jim something—Jean's last name. I had met her, Jay's latest companion, a few months before, and for some reason not knowing her last name bothered me. I was going to call out to Jim, but then I heard his old car grind, catch, and rattle off down Grove Street.

6

Jim and I lived in a working-class neighborhood in Oakland. I had moved there from San Francisco. The storefront was a real find, a place that offered the kind of light and space needed for painting. A friend had built the redwood lofts—one in the studio and one in the back for sleeping. Everything was white, and plants were hung all over from the ceiling and the rafters. It became an oasis, behind the shabby, painted-over storefront on Grove Street. Granted, it had problems. It was drafty. A freeway ramp wound up and over our back yard, and we had to keep a dead bolt on the door. But none of these things bothered me. What did get to me was the idea of renting. I wanted a place of my own. I suppose you could say I wanted to put down roots. Imagine that! Wouldn't that just knock my father for a loop? The idea of his daughter's finally putting down roots.

The phone rang. It was Jay. "Can you meet us at Oakland Airport at ten?" he asked, not wasting words.

I looked at the clock and saw that it was nine. "No problem," I answered, just as tersely. "Where do I go?"

He directed me to the University of California Flying Club hangar. "Turn right on Earhart Road before you get to the main part of the airport."

"Earhart?" I repeated with a mock gulp. "As in Amelia?"

"Right," he said, and I knew he was grinning. "The very one."

"I'll be there," I answered, suddenly feeling very happy about my decision to go along. The desert wildflowers would be in bloom and the air would be fresh and clean. It would be altogether glorious.

I had told Jay it was no problem, but I knew that was not exactly true. I would need to leave in half an hour if I was going to make it on time, and the first thing I had to do was find out if my Karmann Ghia was going to cooperate. I slipped into a down vest and headed out the back door, to the side street where my aging sportscar was parked. It was a

7

sparkling day, so fresh you could almost taste it. Not a day on which to be surrounded by concrete, I thought. The sky was too blue and sunny for that.

"C'mon, Karmann," I said, coaxing, as I fit the key into the ignition. "Be good."

Karmann had no intention of being good. There was a metallic whir, and I knew the battery was dead—one more reason to find a career that would pay. I gave the key another turn, knowing it was hopeless but unable to think of anything else to do. Now I probably couldn't get to the airport on time; I couldn't go flying after all. Disappointment flooded through me. I was surprised at how badly I wanted to go. But maybe Jim could get away from work long enough to drive me. It was a thought. It was worth a try.

It took him a few minutes to get to the phone. I knew that probably meant he was in the middle of something, and I was right. "No way," he said. "But listen, call Jay. He'll be coming from El Sobrante, and it really isn't that much out of his way to pick you up. Ask him. I'm sure he'll do it."

I didn't want to ask Jay to pick me up; he was already doing me a favor by letting me tag along. Maybe he and Jean would just as soon go by themselves. But I had to call him either way, to let him know. I started my explanation awkwardly, and as soon as I got to the dead battery he interrupted.

"We'll swing by to pick you up," he said, "but I'm slow getting it together this morning. We won't be able to get there for another hour—about eleven, I'd guess."

"Great," I answered. "I really appreciate—"

But Jay had no time for thank yous. "Listen," he cut in, "we'll be flying into Furnace Creek and I think I remember some picnic tables there. Would you pack us a lunch?"

"Of course," I answered, happy to be able to do something. My spirits soared; I had another whole hour to get myself dressed and pack a lunch. A quick inventory of the refrigerator turned up half a leftover quiche, peanut butter, cream cheese, jam, and plenty of tangerines. Fine for a desert picnic, I thought. Tangerines for a desert dessert. I giggled.

Then I flew into the closet. It was no ordinary day—no levis and baggy sweater, no down jacket and hiking boots. It was going to be a dress-up day, and I was going to wear what any well-dressed woman would wear to lunch at Furnace Creek. The idea made me laugh, and the cat, warming in the sun, jumped from its perch at the kitchen window and came to rub against my leg.

"Out of my way, cat," I said. "I'm bailing out of here for the day."

I pulled out the suit I had bought in a Los Angeles boutique, the year's big extravagance. The wraparound skirt was a soft beige wool and came to the top of my boots.

Boots. Of course. I scrambled onto the floor of the closet, pushing through the boxes of costumes I had designed for a variety of dramatic productions, and hauled out a pair of russet-brown boots with two-inch heels. A little fancy maybe, but I'd be spending most of the day sitting in the airplane, so they would work. I hung the skirt and matching jacket—a collarless quilted beige wool with a thin blue stripe—on the door while I plunged into a drawer.

A slip; cotton-knit shirt; the new pullover vest I'd bought in Mexico; socks. I pulled out the pair of heavy socks I'd just bought at the Earth Shoe store—bright blue and practical. They should keep my toes warm. I made one last lunge in search of a clean pair of underpants. No luck. I stood there for a minute, contemplating the big basket we used as a clothes hamper. Should I scrounge around and pull out a slightly rumpled pair?

Nope. Not this day. It was dress-up all the way, and you can't wear day-old panties on a dress-up day. I would go bare-assed, and nobody would ever know.

Soon I was scrubbed, brushed, and dressed. I stood in

front of the big mirror for an honest appraisal: tall, a little too thin now, too angular, after having lost fifteen pounds. Hair, curly and clean. That counts; cleanliness counts. I could see the graffiti on the wall: *Lauren Elder doesn't wear underpants.* Beneath that I would write: *Cleanliness counts!*

I put on my glasses and took a harder look. The glasses helped, because the woman in the mirror was quite nearsighted. Now I could see the blue of her eyes, cobalt blue. I wondered why they seemed so serious when the person inside felt so buoyant, so hellbent for a grand day. I wondered if that is why I am told, by people who know me only a little, that I seem a bit cold and distant. What's the phrase they use? "I never know what you're thinking." I wonder why they feel they have to know.

Anyway, the woman in the mirror looked okay. Good skin, good teeth, strong constitution, and—admit it—a good smile. I smiled as a test. It worked.

The pounding on the front door made me jump. I could see Jay's tall figure outlined through the opaque glass, and I could tell by the way he pounded that he wanted to get moving.

2

Most of what I knew about Jay Fuller I knew secondhand, from Jim. Jay ran the vet clinic, which made him Jim's boss as well as his friend. Jay was the kind of man who could manage that, being both a boss and a friend. And it wasn't forced; all the people who worked in the clinic felt good about Jay.

Jay was absorbed in his work, and according to the vets on his staff he was supremely competent. I had heard stories about Jay's fearlessness in surgery, about how he handled animals brought in crushed or broken and bleeding. Jay was the one who took charge, who established priorities. And he was always ready to take calculated risks if he thought they would work.

He had enormous confidence in his own skill; *self-reliant* was the word that kept cropping up when Jay's friends talked about him, as they tended to do. You got the feeling that they

11

trusted him completely, but that they couldn't explain why. Once another vet—a man who knew Jay well—said, "He has this very unsophisticated intelligence." I think that was part of it—the idea that Jay knew something that they didn't, that for all his slow speech, punctuated by long pauses and interspersed with "uhs," he possessed some basic, instinctive intelligence.

He sailed his own boat, flew small planes, rode a motorcycle, and backpacked into the wilderness. There was nothing flashy about the way he did any of those things. He wasn't trying to impress anyone. I guessed that he simply liked living a little closer to the edge than most people.

Jay was, essentially, a farm boy, from some little country town in the West. He was comfortable around animals and machinery; he appreciated raw power. He had gone off to college with one of those souped-up cars, the kind with wide rear tires and a back end that haunches up. He had said that giving up that car had been "a big thing" for him. *A big thing*. I understood that to mean a kind of passage.

Sometime before he had gone off to the veterinary school at UC Davis, Jay had managed a ranch and had done the kinds of chores ranch hands do. It earned him a cowboy reputation. ("You should hear some of Jay's cowboy stories," someone would say, with more than a little awe.) It was the cowboy side of Jay that so intrigued Jim, who grew up in Chicago, the ultimate urban kid.

As far as I could see, only one thing about Jay seemed to bewilder his friends. That was his preference for women much younger than himself. Jay was thirty-six and had been married and divorced twice. Both wives had been quite a bit younger than he. And since he had announced himself beyond marriage, the women he spent time with were usually in their early twenties. One friend had a theory about that. He felt that Jay couldn't manage an equal relationship with a woman. It was the kind of remark you always heard around

Berkeley in the 1970s. A man was defined as macho or not. If he enjoyed the company of much younger women, something had to be wrong with him—some flaw, some deep insecurity.

I thought there might have been another explanation. It seemed to me that at times people tried to read in complexity where there was none. I wondered if the native enthusiasm Jay found in young women more nearly matched his own. But I didn't know Jay Fuller's women very well, and his relationships did not really concern me. I had been to a staff party at his house once and I'd gone on a winter sail on his boat. Aside from that, I suppose I'd seen him half a dozen times, when I would drop by the clinic to see Jim or bring in one of the cats. If I ever had any kind of private conversation with Jay, I can't remember what was said. He saw me as the woman who was involved with Jim. He knew I was off limits, and I liked him for that. But I knew there was something very appealing about him, and I could see why women were so attracted to him.

Standing on my doorstep at eleven on a bright spring morning, smiling, he looked as if he had just gotten out of bed. The lines around his eyes were marked off in puffy little rectangles and triangles. The effect was boyish and somehow charming, as though he had just splashed his face and brushed his teeth and put on a clean shirt but still could not get his eyes quite open.

Jay was over six feet tall and not so much thin as rangy. His full beard was a shade darker than the red of his hair, and he had the classic redhead's coloring: light skin with a sprinkling of pale freckles. He was wearing a nylon windbreaker and jeans.

"Ready?" he said. He didn't want to step inside because that would mean another delay in a morning that was fast disappearing.

I asked him if I needed a jacket and was instantly sorry

13

because I could tell it wasn't the kind of thing he wanted to think about.

"Sure, take one," he answered offhandedly. "I'm planning to be back before dark, but it can get cool crossing the mountains."

The mountains. Of course. I had no idea what mountains he was talking about. The Sierras? The Inyos? The San Bernardinos? There were all kinds of mountain ranges in California. I did know that the few times I'd been in the mountains in the summertime the air had been fresh and cold.

Leaving the door ajar and Jay outside waiting, I gathered up the paper bag with our lunch and the backpack with my Nikon. I struggled into my jacket, grabbing a long silk scarf for my neck and a cap for my ears. It was a slightly ludicrous cap, a brown cotton World War I flying ace kind, complete with ear flaps. I hated the wind in my ears, so the cap—silly or not—might come in handy.

Jean turned to smile as I climbed into the back seat of the Toyota.

"You two've met?" Jay asked.

Jean nodded, but from the shy look she gave me I wasn't sure if she really did remember.

"At the sailing party a couple of months ago," I offered, to refresh her memory. I wasn't sure I'd talked to her at all that day. There had been seven of us on Jay's sailboat, including his daughter, Carla. I remembered that Jean had hovered near him most of that day, while Carla bounced around talking to everyone. A very independent little girl, Carla. She was ten years old and lived with Jay. I wondered how she and Jean got along.

"Did you ever get to go to Mexico?" Jean asked. So she did remember.

"We just got back before Easter," I answered.

Jay swung the car deftly into the traffic at Fifty-first Street, heading across Oakland. "Jean and I took the camper

14

and went to Death Valley at Easter," he said. "That's how we happen to be flying over to Furnace Creek today."

"Jimmie said something about a missing cat," I started.

"Ferocious," Jean put in.

"Ferocious?" I asked.

"That's my house cat," Jay answered for her. "We took him camping with us. I let him out of the camper early one morning and he split. A woman in a trailer camp somewhere near Furnace Creek found him scavenging around in her garbage. He still had his identification tags around his neck, so she called me. I said we'd fly over to pick him up."

"That lady probably thinks he's some kind of cat to have a private plane come for him." Jean laughed.

"He *is* some kind of cat," Jay came back. "He traveled nine miles from the place where we camped. He also gave us a good excuse to fly over to Death Valley for the day."

"The afternoon." Jean corrected him. "But it was nice of that woman to take care of him for you."

"Which reminds me," Jay said, "I want to buy her a gift. Any ideas?"

I waited for Jean to say something. When she didn't, I suggested that a small house plant might work. "A succulent—a cactus maybe?" I said, adding, "Coals to Newcastle?"

Jay grinned. I couldn't imagine him ever laughing out loud, but the grin came easily.

Jean smiled in response. "Good idea," she said. I was glad she hadn't minded my speaking up; I did not want to preempt her.

There was something very wholesome about Jean. She made me think of all the young girls you see on Southern California beaches: girls with fine, sleek bodies in bikinis and waist-length hair bleached by the sun; girls who spend their days climbing in and out of the waves.

Jean's long hair tumbled around her shoulders. It was

15

straight and thick and blonde, and now and then she would brush it back absentmindedly. She was even younger than I had remembered, probably twenty-one or twenty-two. On the sail she had been exceptionally quiet, but now it seemed to me that she probably had just felt uncomfortable around Jay's older friends.

Oakland was, that bright morning, blowing in the wind. Six tall palms in a row were silhouetted against the sun, their fronds tossing wildly. The wind had blown away the haze that often settles over the city in the springtime. That day we would be able to see forever.

Jay must have been thinking the same thing, because he began to hurry, darting in and out of traffic lanes, passing whenever he could.

"Turn in here," I said, directing him into the Rockridge Shopping Center at Fifty-first and Broadway. I knew the Payless Market had a nursery department.

The three of us spilled out of the car and headed for the racks of plants. We must have seemed an unlikely trio—me in my boutique best, boots newly polished; Jay in his sailing garb; and Jean in purest Berkeley funk, with a baggy pair of white overalls, the kind that painters pull over their street clothes. She was tall and nicely shaped, though you couldn't immediately tell it under the bulk of the overalls. Her feet were bare except for a pair of rubber beach sandals, and—a final whimsy—she was wearing oversized sunglasses.

We chose a small, pale green succulent and picked out a pretty little white ceramic pot to put it in. Jay shoved the plant in Jean's hands and took off at a lope toward another store in the mall, while Jean and I waited under the arcade.

"He's going to get a case of beer to take to one of the park rangers," Jean explained. She wasn't quite sure why, but she thought it had something to do with finding the cat.

It would have been a good time to ask her what her last name was, except that would have been admitting that we

16

were, in effect, strangers. It might mar the mood and I didn't want to do that; things were just beginning to get comfortable. I could have inquired about where she lived. (She had said something about a "Nancy," whom I took to be her roommate.) Or I could have asked her where she worked.

In fact, I did none of those things. It no longer seemed to matter. What mattered was getting on with the day, getting airborne. I wanted to view the world from another angle, to sail out and over it, close enough to see the tops of the eucalyptus windbreaks and the patterns made by spring-plowed fields. I wanted to watch cars inch along and I wanted to see rivers glint as they curved like ribbons of light, flashing in the sun. So I didn't ask Jean her last name; and as we stood there in comfortable silence Jay came striding back toward us, cardboard cartons of Olympia beer under each arm, full speed ahead written on his face.

It was nearly 11:30. Jay revved the car, took a quick look in both directions, and shot out of the parking lot through the "in" ramp, onto Pleasant Valley Road. We saved a few seconds but we cut off a woman in an Opel Kadette who, at that precise moment, was leaving the center in the proper lane.

I couldn't believe the coincidence. It was the same woman I'd had my appointment with that morning. Amazing. She had canceled the appointment, and we had just missed careening into her in the Payless parking lot. It occurred to me that there might be a message there, somewhere, but I hadn't the foggiest notion what it was.

"You can take Piedmont Avenue to McArthur," I directed, assuming that this section of Oakland was my turf. I had, in all, gone to thirteen schools in eighteen years—my father had been in the Navy and we had moved a lot—but I had attended high school in Alameda, which adjoins Oakland.

"We can get to the airport by way of 580, can't we?" Jay asked.

17

I said I didn't think so. (Californians tend to talk of freeways in a code. Intersections and connections, all numbered and labeled, flesh out whole conversations.)

"I know there's a way," Jay insisted.

Piedmont Avenue, with all its stops, slowed us down. Jay began to drum on the wheel and make mildly disparaging remarks about drivers who got in his way. Jean and I said nothing.

"McArthur will get us to 580," Jay said again. "There's a cutoff to the airport by Mills College."

I was sure he was wrong but I didn't say so, which was good because it turned out he was right. As soon as we hit the wide boulevard, Jay seemed to relax.

"Jimmie says you've got a new partner," I said. I was curious to hear just what was happening at the clinic Jay managed. I knew there was tension between the owners, who were pushing for bigger profits, and Jay and the staff, who wanted to practice good veterinary medicine for what they considered to be fair rates.

"Right," Jay answered. "A really good vet. His name is Milligan." He laughed then, a self-deprecating little laugh. "By good I mean we practice the same kind of medicine, or at least we have the same ideas about it." He added, "We'd like to buy the clinic and run it the way it should be run, making money without ripping anybody off. But whatever happens, I think things are going to work out well."

"That's great," I told him. "Jimmie told me about the hassles with the owners. I hope you can get free of them."

Now and then Jean and Jay would have exchanges that did not include me. I was glad for the chance to sit back and be separate. I didn't have to make polite conversation. They were together and I was along for the ride; it had been nicely established. Now he was telling her which local station to tune in to for a weather report, and Jean was busy with the radio.

"San Francisco Bay Area weather," the voice boomed out. "Fair through Tuesday, slightly warmer Tuesday. Highs today in the sixties near the coast and low seventies inland." The words rolled out in a familar cadence. "Small craft advisory is in effect for San Francisco Bay, including Suisun Bay and the West Delta. North-to-northwest winds fifteen to thirty miles per hour. And if any of you folks are heading for the mountains, well, the word is there are winds from thirty to fifty miles per hour, with a traveler's advisory for strong, gusty winds. There may even be some showers on the eastern slopes." The announcer's voice slipped back into a normal tone. Jean switched off the radio as we turned onto Earhart Road.

At the Flight Services Building Jay jumped out, saying he'd only be a minute.

"He has to fill out the usual forms and stuff," Jean told me, "and find out about the weather where we're going. The plane's reserved, so we'll be able to go right away." She busied herself loading film into an Instamatic.

I had been trying to ignore the small, persistent signals that I had to go to the bathroom. Now I realized, chagrined, that I needed to make a stop and I hoped I'd have a chance. Otherwise I would have to wait until we reached Death Valley, and that, I knew, would be miserable.

Jay came out, trying to fold a giant map that was flapping in the wind. "The word is gusty but clear," he told us. "We'll be on our way by noon. It's probably going to be rough."

"What's the forecast?" I asked, as if I hadn't heard.

He went into more detail. "There are aviation wind warnings—strong northerly winds with gusts over thirty knots—but it's clear, with good visibility." He didn't seem perturbed by either the weather or my question.

Loaded with packages, we headed for the Cal Flying Club hangar. Jay shifted the beer to one hip while he unlocked the outer door and led us into a dingy anteroom, the kind of place where people pass through but never stop. He had already unlocked the next door and was holding it for us when I noticed a door marked "Men" (underneath which someone had scrawled "Women" and someone else "Persons"). I told myself I could wait, because I knew that Jay was pushing to get off. He wanted to get over the mountains as early as possible, he said. I wanted to ask him why but I didn't, since he might have thought I was questioning his judgment. We went through the hangar, passing several planes in various stages of disassembly, and walked out into the area next to the airstrip, where the planes were moored.

The glare of sun on the white concrete apron hit us full face. It was so bright that it hurt. Jean squinted and cupped her free hand over her eyes. Only Jay seemed not to notice; he was scanning the field for our aircraft.

"It's a Cessna 182," he said, as if Jean and I should be able to recognize it. Then he spotted the plane and started off, the two of us in his wake.

We were heading for a little red-and-white plane that was bobbing in its moorings. The wind rising off the bay swept across the open expanse of field and the concrete runways. Long marsh grass was blowing to the ground. It was not cold, but the wind was strong.

Jean lifted the empty cat cage she was carrying into the baggage compartment behind the back seat. Then Jay and I stowed our packages while Jean climbed into the front seat. She began to rummage through her handbag. Jay had an official-looking list of things which he said had to be routinely checked before any flight. I asked if I could tag after him. I knew I'd be sitting for a long while, and I was beginning to feel restless.

"You've been in small planes before?" he asked. When I said not really, that actually I'd been up only twice before, he said, "Oh. I thought Jim said your father was a pilot."

I never knew how to respond to that, what to say about my father. I did not want to be rude, but I also did not want to go into a litany about my father's background. "He is. He was in the Navy," I answered, adding, "mostly testing jets."

It seemed to satisfy Jay, or maybe it was just that he was so preoccupied with the inspections that he didn't say more. Whatever the reason, I was glad. He moved quickly around the plane, ducking under the wing, squatting to look at the tires. I walked behind him, asking questions which he answered perfunctorily.

The plane seemed so small. I stared at the tires. "They're like wheelbarrow tires," I said, "so toylike."

"They do the job," Jay answered.

I reached up to touch the window through which I would be taking photographs. "Yuck," I commented involuntarily. My finger left a mark in the thick layers of accumulated dirt.

"Yeah, it's pretty dirty," Jay remarked. "It looks like it's just about due for a hundred-hour inspection. That's when they wash it." I must have looked worried, because he quickly added, "It's FAA regulations. They're very strict about safety."

Suddenly I blurted, "Did you file a flight plan?"

The question was too abrupt, but Jay didn't seem to notice. "No," he said, shrugging. "It's not really necessary. It's not required."

He stood back so I could climb into the rear seat. Then he swung into the pilot's seat the way he might have swung onto a horse. He began the instrument check at once.

I realized I was not going to be able to wait until Death Valley to go to the toilet. I squeezed my legs together, disgusted with my rebellious bladder. Jay was getting ready to take off and I had to go to the bathroom in the worst way. I asked myself how old you have to be before you stop getting yourself into these predicaments—or at least learn how to get yourself out of them.

21

Jean had been talking to Jay, interrupting his checkout and obviously annoying him. She was wheedling, arguing mildly. He shook his head but she persisted, still shielding her eyes from the glare of the field. Finally Jay lifted himself out of his seat, dug into the pocket of his jeans, and handed her some keys; he resumed his checkout at once.

"My sunglasses," Jean called to me. "I left them in the car." With that she was off and running and I was right behind her, more glad than she could possibly know for the excuse.

I darted into the toilet and was finished by the time Jean got back with her glasses. "I'd better go too," she said.

I stood waiting for Jean in the empty corridor. Suddenly I felt a need to *move,* to release some energy. I did a small, controlled spin that I'd learned in my karate class. In midair, something in the center of me constricted.

Don't go.

The message was clear enough.

Or was it?

What is this message business anyway? I asked myself. Then I tried to be practical. How could I not go? How would I get home, for starters? There probably weren't any buses this far out. I'd have to walk along the freeway. And what would I say to Jay and Jean? They'd gone out of their way to pick me up; I'd delayed them enough already. They would think I was a righteous nut. Besides, it would cast a pall over their trip.

And what is a premonition? Do the clouds have to part and the voice of God rain down on you?

Maybe I could tell them I felt sick. It would be a lie, and I was not good at lying. Anyway, that would be a weak way out. If you don't go you say no, flat out: *Sorry folks, thanks a whole lot. It's been nice, but so long, it's been good to know you.*

I didn't know them, not really. Maybe if I had, I could

have gotten out of it more easily. The fear was there, all right, a small, tight knot in my stomach. But was it really a premonition? Right now the airport—any airport in the whole country—was probably filled with people telling themselves: *Don't get on that plane.* How dumb.

I remembered a story that a TWA pilot once told me. He had been flying east and had run into engine trouble, so he made an emergency stop at Cincinnati or someplace like that. The mechanical problem was fixed, and everyone began to reboard to continue the flight. One of the passengers, a priest, stepped up to the pilot and said, "I've been thinking that the engine trouble was a sign, and I think that perhaps I shouldn't continue the trip." All the other passengers stood there, waiting to see what the captain would say. "Well, Father," he answered, "maybe you did get a sign that says you should stay, but the sign I got is to get home to Rochester tonight, and that's just what I'm going to do." So everybody got back on the plane, and they all arrived safely in Rochester.

Jean hurried out of the bathroom, her eyes shining with excitement. I took a deep breath and smiled back at her. The two of us then ran out through the hangar and onto the concrete. In the meantime, Jay had contacted the tower and was getting instructions for takeoff. The plane was quivering and ready to roll as we climbed in, breathless and laughing.

3

"Good thinking," Jay shouted over his shoulder. He was referring to my window cleaning. Before jumping into the plane I had managed to swab off the gritty rear window with the paper towels I brought from the toilet. Then, as we taxied to the runway, the plane shuddering as crosswinds caught it, I had cleaned the inside of one rear window and slid across the back seat to clean the other. The seat was a kind of bench, padded in plastic, great for sliding on. I was glad to have it to myself, so I could take pictures out of both rear windows.

"You should be able to get some great shots today. It's as clear as I've ever seen it," Jay called to me over the roar of the engine.

Jay listened through the headset as the control tower radioed instructions; then he relayed them to us. "We'll be taking off toward downtown Oakland."

I snapped on the seatbelt and swallowed a few times. I always do that on takeoffs, partly to keep my ears from popping and partly out of nervousness. Inevitably, during the pause at the end of the runway, some neon light flashes in my brain: *Most crashes happen on takeoff and landing.*

Then we were hurtling ahead, gaining speed, the plane vibrating wildly in the wind and noise. I braced my arm against a wall and was surprised to feel it give—the wall was padded too. *Well*, I told myself, *you're all dressed up and settled into this nice little padded compartment, so sit back and enjoy the ride. You have reached the point of no return.*

"We're up," Jay called out.

Jean smiled and said, "I noticed—and it's only noon too."

The runway was no more than a glare of sun on concrete; white caps flecked the bay. The air cushioned and buffeted us at the same time, so that the plane rolled from side to side, the right wing tilting first and then the left in a jerking, rolling dip. I concentrated on keeping my stomach in place.

I lifted my camera as a gust of wind tossed us up, then dropped us just as suddenly.

"Whoops," Jean said nervously.

"As soon as we make this turn the wind will be at our back and things will get smoother," Jay assured us.

I moved as close to the window as I could, pressing my forehead against the glass, trying to identify buildings. "What's that?" I asked, pointing to a futuristic, raw concrete shape.

Jay looked. "It could be Chabot College," he replied. "You want me to circle so we can see?"

"No," I said, "no need."

Jay was more animated than I had believed he could be, sitting in the cockpit, his hand on the stick, moving us through space.

"Look at that," Jean cried out. The salt flats that edge into San Francisco Bay appeared as great, exquisite geometric

25

shapes, a sulfurous yellow juxtaposed against a deep carmine. The colors caught my breath and I thought, as I do every time I fly into San Francisco International or Oakland: *If only I could get those exact shades on canvas.*

When we wheeled and turned the ride became smoother, just as Jay had promised. *It's like riding a horse,* I thought. *You have to relax and commit yourself to the movement, the flow.* Looking at Jay, I more nearly understood what my mother meant when she said she could always tell when my dad had been flying or when I had been horseback riding. "You would come back so *clear,*" my mother would say.

Now San Francisco and the Pacific were behind us. We were heading south and east, toward the low-lying Coast Range. The rounded hills of the range were the softest greens and browns imaginable, so sensuous and velvety that I wanted to put my hand down to caress them. Occasionally there were oak trees nestled like tufts of fur into the folds of the hills, or newly plowed fields that looked like pieces of corduroy.

I shuffled through my shoulder bag and came up with a pen and a rumpled piece of paper good enough to sketch a design on. The pattern below made me think of doing a landscape quilt, one that could be executed in greens and browns, with bits of velvet and corduroy. I could see that my sketch would work. The translation from earth to design pleased me and I felt a sudden surge of energy. The day was turning out to be an esthetic joy.

Jean turned to offer me a peppermint. Through her big, funny glasses I could see how thrilled she was. "Isn't this terrific?" she said, bubbling.

I said yes, it was unbelievably beautiful.

"You ain't seen nothin' yet," Jay drawled, teasing, obviously pleased that we were pleased. "Wait until you get your first look at the High Sierra. Now *that* is something."

I knew Jay had been flying for about six years and I knew

he and Jim had flown over the mountains before on a mid-winter trip to the hot springs near Mammoth.

"How long before we see the mountains?" Jean asked.

Jay studied the aeronautical chart that was spread out on his lap. "A little more than an hour," he answered vaguely.

I had unsnapped my seatbelt so I could slide around to get the best angle. Sometimes I would forget all about the camera in my fascination with a lake, the light glinting off it like a mirror, flashing out to us. Or I would watch a tiny car winding ever so slowly, in concentric circles, up a mountain road. Now and then a gust of wind would toss us to one side, but I quickly learned how to brace myself. I was glad for the cushioned back seat, since there was nothing much to bump against. By comparison Jean and Jay seemed cramped in their pilot's seats.

In no time at all we had passed over the Coast Range and were into the Central Valley, the southern part of which is called the San Joaquin. Most Californians call it the Big Valley, and that's what it is, all right. It is the very core of the state.

There was an amazing kind of order to the land that stretched out below us. The fields—flat and wide and marked off by precise stripes—seemed to reach to infinity. I knew the stripes were roads traveled by pickup trucks going eighty miles an hour, leaving plumes of dust behind them, hellbent for wherever. From 31,000 feet in a jet this is just another monotonous valley, but at 3,500 feet in a little Cessna it is something else entirely. Its sweeping, rectangular order registers on you—this vast green grid where tourists hardly ever go.

Jay was sitting with the map spread on his lap; Jean did not seem to be involved in the navigating. They chatted now and then, Jean leaning across the space between them. I realized that in the several hours we had been together I had not seen

27

them touch. I wondered how close Jay would let any woman get to him. It was an idle thought. I didn't really care. The one thing that was clear was that the valley was not enough for him; he was anxious to get into the mountains.

"What's that lake?" Jean asked.

"Some reservoir," he answered, looking at the map but not finding a name. "Looks low."

Jean reminded him that there had been little rain the past winter.

"It'll be interesting to see how much snow is in the mountains," he replied.

Snow. I hadn't thought about snow, but of course there would still be a pack in the mountains. It would probably be downright cold when we passed over them. Suddenly I envied Jean's big down jacket. I wished I had brought mine along, but at home it had seemed so out of place. I wondered why Jay had been so offhanded about taking warm clothes. But he had made this trip before, and he was wearing only a light nylon windbreaker over a cotton shirt. I supposed the heater in the plane would take care of the chill.

Once again Jay offered to circle if I saw anything I wanted to photograph, and again I declined. I was anxious to get into the mountains too.

"Will we by flying over Yosemite?" I asked, having finally realized that Yosemite had to be somewhere to the east of us.

"We're already south of Yosemite," Jay answered. "We'll cross the Sierras in Kings Canyon National Park—you know, the John Muir Trail."

I didn't know, but I didn't say so.

Then Jay added, "It's really rugged country."

The sun was high overhead now. It was midday and we were floating along, saying little to one another, although now and then Jay or Jean would point out something. I kept my eyes on the earth and thought about the first time I'd been

28

in a small plane. I was about twelve at the time. My father was the pilot and I was his only passenger; we were going from our home in Maryland to Williamsburg, Virginia. I don't remember why we were going there, or why my mother and my younger brother, Craig, drove instead of flying with us. But I know it was a plane like the Cessna, and I was sitting in the front, next to my father. The sky was full of dark clouds. There was thunder and lightning and rain and we were being tossed up and down.

I was scared, but I knew my father was not. Just the opposite: He was excited by the storm. So despite my fear I felt safe. I had always felt safe with my father. In those days he was testing jets, but I never worried about him. It never occurred to me that he could die, though I knew that other test pilots he knew had died. My parents would go over to someone's house and then there would be another widow in their circle of friends.

My family tells a story about my father and me. I've heard it often enough to think that I even remember the event itself, but I couldn't, since I wasn't quite three at the time. We were living in Coronado, the naval base in San Diego. (We would be back at the base again in our peregrinations around the country.) My father was watering the lawn, and I began to play a game with him. I would turn the water off, run around the corner, and watch to see what he did when the water trickled out of the hose and stopped. He told me once not to do it and then told me again, the second time more firmly. My father is a big man—well over six feet tall—and not at all used to having his orders disobeyed. The third time I went around the corner to watch him he came after me. I must have seen that he was angry because I broke and ran. I scooted through a gate and let it swing shut. The gate caught my father full in the face and broke his nose.

Sometimes I think my family tells this story because it shows the way my father and I were for a long time: me challenging, goading; he reacting as if hit full in the face. It is no longer that way, but that is only recently.

"Fresno coming up soon," Jay called out, bringing me back to the present. "Then we'll swing into the mountains."

We hit a small bump and lurched.

"How high will we be going?" Jean asked.

"Way up. We'll be crossing north of Mt. Whitney, and that's 14,000 feet."

"Whew!" I said, suddenly sobered. "That's high. Do you do that often?"

Jay grinned. "Often enough." His voice said it was routine; his voice said not to sweat it. "Let's see what's going on up there," he added, fiddling with the instruments. "Fresno radio, this is Cessna N52855 at 9,000 feet traveling east, destination Furnace Creek. Request weather en route." It was a kind of drone—a radio voice, I decided.

There was a long pause while he listened: then he relayed the information to us. "Clear—thirty miles' visibility—moderate to severe turbulence below 20,000 feet."

"Will we be flying below 20,000 feet?" Jean asked.

Jay grimaced and said yes. He explained that the plane wasn't built to travel higher than 20,000 feet—and neither were any of us, at least not for long.

Jean looked puzzled.

"Oxygen," he said. "You couldn't breathe very well at 20,000."

"Will we have trouble breathing at 14,000?" I asked.

"You'll notice it some, but we won't be up that high very long, no more than ten or fifteen minutes. Then we'll come down again. The air is pretty rare."

Jean asked if it was going to be rough, and Jay said that it probably would be choppy, but it was nothing to worry about.

Fresno disappeared under our right wing as the suburbs gave way to the fields. We could see the curving patterns, the

30

cul-de-sacs, the houses, each with a little car. It occurred to me that subdivisions look more interesting from the air than they do from the ground. The design of the whole is better than any of its parts. I smiled at my own equation.

At about one o'clock—I figured we'd been airborne for an hour or so—Jay started a low turn. The sky was perfectly still, and before I really noticed we were in a climb. Suddenly, the foothills of the majestic Sierras surged at us.

"There they are," Jay called out. "Now the real fun begins."

4

At eight o'clock on the morning of December 7, 1941, my mother was standing on a hillside in Honolulu overlooking Pearl Harbor. Japanese planes flew over that hill on their way to the harbor, and she had a clear view of them. She could see the red zeros painted on the sides and could even see the pilots. She watched the bombs drop, watched as smoke began to rise from the crippled battleships. It seemed, she told me once, like something that was taking place far away. She felt peculiarly removed from the enormity of what was happening that balmy Sunday morning in Hawaii. She had no sense of imminent danger and was not afraid. The night before, she had been out with a young ensign from the *Arizona*. He would die that morning.

Sometimes I think of my mother as she must have been then, a tiny, exuberant woman of twenty-two, standing on a hillside on Oahu. I imagine her in a fresh, flower-sprigged cotton dress, perfectly starched by the Japanese woman who did the laundry for the young secretaries who came from the mainland. Some of the other young women left after the bombing of Pearl Harbor, but my mother wasn't ready to go home to Spokane. She and her roommates rented a bungalow on the beach at Waikiki, and she spent the first year of the war there.

My father was an ensign, a fighter pilot of Bomber Squadron Three flying off the *Enterprise,* the *Yorktown,* or the *Saratoga.* He arrived in Honolulu after the bombing of Pearl Harbor. In a box of family photographs there is one of my mother and father on their wedding day: October 23, 1942, Honolulu. She is wearing a tailored white suit with a little veiled hat, and he is in his full summer dress whites. He towers over her. They look terribly young, and it is very romantic.

My father saw action the first two years of the war and collected several medals, none of which I have heard him mention. But my mother had them matted on velvet, and they hang in the study of their house in Palos Verdes, along with the other memorabilia of his military career: the plaque that says he was captain of the carrier *Coral Sea,* the awards and citations that describe him as a pioneer in aviation.

My father was one of the first men to fly a jet off an aircraft carrier. Flying is at the center of his life and always has been. And so, in a way, has it been the center of my mother's.

He is fifty-seven now, my father. Not long ago my mother told me that he has outlived his life expectancy. Experimental test pilots are high risks. She mentioned it in passing, as something of interest. Statisticians, or whoever makes up life expectancy charts, did not think my father would still be around today. Well, he fooled them, but he didn't fool me. They do not know my father; they could not possibly understand his tenacity. My father is too willful to die.

33

When I was an adolescent I would say things like that to him, would taunt him, and he would be furious. We slammed against each other in those years, one of us as determined as the other not to back off. The power struggles between us were painful beyond description. I came of age in the 1960s; it was inevitable that my father and I found ourselves sharply opposed on the issues of that decade. We clashed, again and again. It took me a long time to understand that those years, those clashes, were as wounding for him as they were for me. It took me even longer to understand how alike we are, my father and I.

I spent half of my growing-up years on the East Coast, half on the West. When I finished high school in Southern California I was determined to go east to college. I finally chose Swarthmore and decided to study international relations. It seemed, in the mid-1960s, a reasonable way to make an impact on the world. But by the end of my second year at Swarthmore I had a vague feeling that international relations was wrong for me. About that time my father flew east for a business trip—one of his regular jaunts to Washington—and he came to Pennsylvania to see me. By then he had left the Navy and was working for an aircraft manufacturer. It was a perfunctory visit, the ritual forty-five-minute tour of the campus. I told him I wanted to go back to the West Coast and enroll in Berkeley or UCLA. He agreed. Then later, when I said I wanted to switch to art, he said, "Yes, fine." I was surprised that he backed those decisions. This, though, was before I understood that I am very much his daughter.

I was thinking about my parents as Jay and Jean and I approached the Sierras. Almost without warning, the foothills became mountains. These were real mountains, higher and wilder than any I'd ever seen, and somehow more spectacular. I had crossed the Swiss Alps once in a car, but it was not the same, not like flying low through a mountain valley in a small plane. The terrain below us was wooded and utterly empty. It was the emptiness—the vast, quiet solitude—that caught and held me.

I thought: *This is what they mean by "wilderness."* The word took on a new dimension. From that time it would conjure for me a scene of conifers—erect, pointing to the sky, like thousands of black slashes on a white background, layer upon layer, moving up the mountains. It would make me think of great gray boulders sprinkled like pebbles over a mountainside, of water rushing and wind blowing and a great, leaden, gray silence. Below us lay the mountains in winter, cold and closed, formidable, forbidding. I shivered and asked Jay to turn on the heater.

"Oh, sure," he said. "This should help."

It didn't. I pulled on my wool jacket and rubbed my hands together. Jean had taken out her Instamatic and was quickly snapping pictures. She had not put on her down jacket, and Jay looked comfortable in his light windbreaker. They seemed impervious to the chill.

Below us one range gave way to the next as we worked our way into deeper wilderness. I saw no cabins, not even a road in the tangle below. There was snow in all the valleys, deep, drifted snow—much more than I had expected. Only the windswept ridges and flanks of the peaks were clear. In the early afternoon sun the shadows of the conifers fell blue on the white of the snow. We flew for miles into this primitive world. It was so different from what I had imagined—wilder and colder and more harshly beautiful—and I lost all notion of time.

As if to emphasize my awe, we took a deep elevator dip, and I instinctively reached behind the seat with both arms to get a good grip. Luckily the back of the seat was open, so I could reach far behind into the baggage section. Once or twice the unexpected rolls made me consider putting on my seatbelt, but each time I decided against it. The view was so grand I didn't want to limit myself to one side window.

I had had trepidations during takeoff, but in the mountains I was too enthralled to be afraid. It was turbulent, yet there was so much to keep my mind occupied. And once I had become accustomed to the dips and plunges, I felt a kind of thrill at our daring. Jay was having a wonderful time, slipping the little plane through these valleys and massive mountains, acting like a guide to two thoroughly engrossed women. We were safe, invulnerable inside our little cocoon. The wilderness was out there, in that great, empty, cold space beyond the skin of the airplane. We would be home in time for supper.

But the Cessna continued to shudder and bob, and every now and then, when the wind seemed to be assuming control, I would glance at Jay for reassurance. His shoulders were relaxed, and I could see he was in control. He would be pointing something out to Jean, but I couldn't hear him. The engine noise seemed to increase as we went higher. My ears were popping in the unpressurized craft, and that made hearing even more difficult.

After a while Jay turned and shouted to me, "Wait until you get your first glimpse of the crest."

"How far?" I shouted back, but he didn't hear me.

For a time I concentrated on a small, high cloud, or rather on the shadow it cast on the valley below. *Poor cloud,* I thought, *so insignificant in such an immense blue sky.* At that moment it seemed impossible ever to imagine enough clouds to fill that intense blueness.

I slid from one side of the seat to the other, shooting rapidly, trying to get it on film. As we moved deeper into the mountain wilderness we seemed to be flying lower, though I knew that was an illusion. The mountains were getting higher, and some peaks were rising above us. I could make out the details of individual trees, could almost see their branches and clusters of needles. Now and then the light would seem to single out one tree and catch its branches blowing in the wind. The whole tree would become incandescent, shimmering, moving.

I thought of the flowers back in Oakland, daffodils and camellias and rhododendrons flowing over every lawn. Spring was well advanced in Oakland; cherry trees had already flowered and were full of new growth. Yet in the Sierras, even at lower elevations, winter's hand was still heavy.

But there were signs that the spring thaw had begun, that this land was coming out of its deep freeze. I glimpsed a waterfall, liquid snow roaring and falling free, plunging hundreds of feet into the dense green, throwing out its spray like a misty veil caught in the wind. It seemed to me I could hear its roar, the only sound in this vast silence other than the hum of our engine.

I thought: *If only I could paint that waterfall, really express it—every essential aspect of it. If I could capture on canvas the tremendous sense of power, the living quality, the surging motion. If I could translate all those qualities into two dimensions and yet preserve the power.*

The waterfall slipped away under the right wing, and then we were moving into still higher mountains. We had climbed well above the tree line; below us we could see only the forbidding rocks, gray and glinting in the cold light. Snow lay in all the crevasses, drifted and solid. I had no idea how high we were; I knew only that it was cold and that I was growing uncomfortable as the cold began to seep into our little craft. I rummaged into my bag and found my World War I flying ace cap and pulled it on, letting the flaps hang loose so it wouldn't seem quite so outlandish. Jean glanced back and did a quick doubletake when she saw my headgear. Then she giggled nicely and smiled, and I smiled back at her.

It got rougher as we climbed, and now Jay seemed to be

concentrating on the flying. I could see that we were in a canyon and that it forked into a **Y**. We followed the southern branch. There was plenty of space between us and the mountains; we were in the open and the views were superb. I kept my camera focused out the side window.

Jay called back to me, "We'll cross at Kearsarge Pass."

I thought: *If you say so*. I had never heard of Kearsarge Pass, but the name had a nice ring to it. I wondered if it had any connection with the man the aircraft carrier *Kearsarge* was named for; I thought he might have been one of those incredible pioneers who made it over these mountains before the turn of the century. Looking at the snow and the steep terrain, I marveled that any person could cross it in winter. It seemed too wild and too harsh for anyone to attempt.

I had always visualized mountain passes as significant chasms between quite separate peaks. I had imagined the Sierra crest to be a line of mountains, each with a valley in between. It wasn't like that at all. Ahead of us I could see a towering granite wall, a single, great ridge with only a few concave places in it, low points so insignificant they were hard to pick out. One of these was Kearsarge Pass.

"Mt. Whitney's over there in that group somewhere," Jay said, waving an arm to the south.

Jean and I dutifully looked to where he pointed, but we couldn't possibly tell which mountain he meant. At 14,495 feet, Mt. Whitney is the highest point along this stretch of the High Sierra, but it is only one of many peaks above the 14,000-foot level.

It suddenly dawned on me that there was no way for our little airplane to get to the other side of the mountains except to go over them. Over the top. I had thought we might just scoot through a valley, but there was none. There was no way to go but up.

Jay looked at the map on his lap and then shouted, "There's Kearsarge."

38

I couldn't figure out how he could know. He was pointing to what seemed a very little declivity in the mass of mountains before us. I was glad that he was sure about where he was going, glad that he seemed so excited about the prospect of clearing these awesome mountains. I was glad because this was a critical point in our journey, and I needed to know that the pilot could handle hard reality.

For a while we seemed to be flying low. We were in a tight valley with walls on both sides. I tried to picture how we must look from the mountaintop above us. Suddenly I had the sensation that we were in a B-movie, the kind with that ghastly color they call "natural"; we were in a sequence with what was obviously a dummy plane, floating in a phony environment. It was not real, that clumsy, bobbing little model airplane and the background music soaring and moaning.

"Get ready for a fantastic view when we clear the crest," Jay shouted back to me. "There's going to be a desert valley on the other side."

I looked at Jean. We smiled a "here we go" kind of smile and returned to our cameras and our windows, not wanting to miss a single moment, knowing that we were committed now and that the climax, the highest part, was going to be the most exciting. I pushed myself into it. I wanted to cram every image possible into my head and as many as I could into the camera. I looked out the back window to see how far we had come and I gasped. The panorama of mountains that spread in great waves behind us caught and held me. I was transfixed by the sight; I was reminded of my insignificance; I was overcome.

Jay shouted, "Hang-on, you're going to feel a big jolt as we clear the crest. We'll drop with the air currents."

My God, my seatbelt! I hadn't buckled my seatbelt, and now there was no time. No time.

I dropped my camera at the same time that I turned to look out the front window, turned to see the wall of granite rise in

39

front of us. Solid, hard, no sky. I could see the veins in the rocks, so close. My God.

I looped my arms over the back of the seat while images flashed across my mind-screen: *Go limp. Drunks survive, sleeping people survive. Hold on tight.* The noise from within matched the noise without and we hit—oh, my God, we hit—so hard.

Metal against metal, muffled; a scraping, a crunching, and a grinding. Not loud; too close to be loud.

And then everything was profoundly still.

Then there was no sound at all.

5

The gash was deep. Layers of flesh parted, neatly, to reveal the unmistakable glistening whiteness of bone and gristle.

My bone.

My gristle.

No blood flowed from the wound. It was precise, almost surgical, and it was on my right leg just above the boottop, a long and deep gash. I looked at it dispassionately, for some time, as if the leg belonged to somebody else. I knew very well it was my flesh ripped open. But I felt no pain, no alarm, no emotion at all. At the same time, I was certain that I was *all right*. I didn't think it. I just knew it. It was like a stop-motion sequence in a movie. The action freezes on a single frame and holds. There is no sound, only a thick, ominous silence; then the camera rolls again and the action hurtles forward, inexorably.

The door snapped open and my camera fell out. I reacted,

grabbing at it, clambering out of the plane. The cold hit me full in the face—stunning, shocking. I slipped on a loose rock but I got to the camera.

As I was bending over to pick it up, Jay bellowed, "Forget the goddamn camera!"

I looked at him and reeled. "My God, Jay—your face!" My voice was a whisper. His face was covered with blood. There was an open wound in his head but it had stopped bleeding. The blood that covered his face had dried, forming a crust that resembled a demon mask. I didn't want to look at him but I had to; my eyes locked on his face.

"Jean's unconscious," he barked. "Get around to the other door and help me get her out."

"But your face," I protested.

"Forget my face; just help me with Jean."

Help him with Jean. Right. I had my orders. That's all I had to think about, getting around the plane and climbing up to the other door. Jay was telling me what to do. I had to move.

The plane was caught on the mountain only fifteen feet short of the crest—no more than the width of a room! It had burrowed into the granite rubble and had turned, slightly, so that it was not quite perpendicular to the ridge. The left wingtip was buried on the downslope side; the other lifted into the air. The nose was pointed obliquely toward the crest. The tail section had cracked open, leaving a space exposed to the sky, but it remained attached to the body of the plane.

The Cessna was upright, at least, but we were on the top of the world. There was nothing up that high but cold and rock, a mixture of small and large boulders, one on top of the other, the crumbling exterior of this solid granite mass. Many of the rocks were loose and the incline was steep, so I could not stand upright and keep my balance. I had to test each rock to see if it offered solid footing, the way I might test rocks at the seashore. Except that here the penalty for slipping was not a splash in the ocean but a headlong plunge down the mountain.

Still, I had a mission: to reach Jean. I concentrated on each footstep, moving carefully in the space between rocks when I could, avoiding shards of glass from the plane. Exploded glass was everywhere. I looked at it as I had looked at the gash on my leg, not knowing how it had happened or when or how I could have missed it. Just as I had missed seeing the blood flow from the wound on Jay's face. I must have been unconscious for a time.

With each step I gasped for breath, unable to fill my lungs. For a while I tried breathing in shallow intakes, the cold stinging my lungs even as I gulped for more air. Gas was leaking from a spigot under the downslope wing. I stood for a long minute looking at the slow, steady trickle, and the smell caught in my nostrils.

"Hurry!" Jay urged.

I wanted to call out that I was coming, but I couldn't. My chest ached too much to say anything.

I climbed from one rock to the next. It seemed to take forever to get the few feet to the front of the plane. I stopped to look at the propeller. *My God,* I thought. *Look at that.* It was bent into a crazy twist. I stared at it, trying to put it in place. Then something happened inside me.

This is it, I thought; *this has happened.*
We won't be home for supper.
We can't go back and do it over again.
There is no second chance. This is done.
We have crashed on the mountaintop.

As the realization struck me, I lifted my eyes and for the first time took in the panorama that lay at my feet, a vast and uncompromising wilderness, an alien place not meant for human life. I looked at the sharp, saw-toothed pinnacles above us on either side and realized that we had crashed just below the peaks of what had to be two of the highest mountains in the Sierras. I looked west from where we had come and thought of all that lay between us and help.

And then I remembered the gas dripping under the wing. The plane could explode. It could boil up into the sky in a funnel of fire and smoke. There would be a roar and a rush of air. We had to get Jean out of there, fast.

Dear God, help me move.

I wanted to rush but I couldn't. My legs would not do as I directed. I couldn't get enough air into my lungs, and the rocks would not yield to speed. It was like a nightmare in which you know you must act quickly, that all will be lost if you do not hurry, that your very life depends on quick action, and it is impossible. Something held me back, something heavy. I was in slow motion and could not shake myself fully awake.

The metal on the airplane was cold and my fingers were stiff. I wanted to curse them for refusing to obey my commands. I struggled with the door handle. When I got it to turn I fought to lift it. It would not budge. I was infuriatingly weak, but I had to get it open. I had to. I threw all my weight against it and finally it gave.

Jean was held in place by her seatbelt. Her body slumped toward the lower door where Jay crouched, waiting.

"Unfasten her seatbelt," he directed from below.

It was not going to be easy. Jean weighed more than I did, and she was totally limp. I held on to the rough cloth of her overalls while I tugged at the belt. It wouldn't release. Jay crawled in on the other side and tried to help. He was moving slowly and awkwardly, and I thought: *What's wrong with us?*

I wanted to ask him if he was all right, but I had to concentrate on Jean. I braced my head against hers to keep it from bumping; her long, silky blonde hair poured out over us. Then I gave her seatbelt a hard tug and it came loose. My arms were around her, and I guided her to Jay, who fumblingly lowered her out the door.

She was unconscious. I watched as he tried to settle her on the rocks. For a long moment the two of them balanced precariously and I was sure they would fall down the mountain in a slide of rocks and bodies. The terrain was all boulders. He could find no flat area and finally allowed her to slump on the massive rocks. Then Jay leaned back, exhausted.

I remembered the gasoline. "Jay!" I shouted. "There's a gas leak under the wing. The plane could explode!"

He looked at me and blinked, as if the meaning of what I said had not seeped in. It was a peculiar sensation. I felt that we were curiously out of synchronization.

"No, it won't explode," he said. His speech was measured, wooden. "Get back around here. Help me. Jean's unconscious. We've got to keep her warm."

I was relieved to hear that the plane wouldn't explode, relieved that Jay knew what we should do and that he would tell us—Jean and me—when she came to. He had the medical training; he knew about airplanes and wilderness. Jay had the right answers.

As I picked my way back around the wing, I realized my mouth was full of gravel. I thought: *How in the world?* I spat it out on the rocks and was surprised to see bits of white. It wasn't gravel after all. It was fragments of teeth. I ran my tongue around my mouth; it caught on snags and broken points. Some of my teeth were shattered! My tongue pained terribly. I realized I had bitten it in the back and that one of my molars was split in two.

Okay, I said to myself with a strange efficiency. *Time to assess the damage.* There was a warm, sticky feeling between my legs. I was bleeding from the vaginal area, but it wasn't heavy and I figured it couldn't be bad. The gash on my leg looked gruesome, but it didn't pain me and didn't seem to impede me much. *Okay.* The strangest sensation came from my left forearm. When I twisted it I could feel something move inside—something that wasn't supposed to

45

move, I was sure of it. But I could still wiggle my fingers, and if I didn't twist the arm I could use my hand.

Jay was crouching next to Jean, waiting for me. "We've got to keep her warm," he repeated. "Stay with her while I get her jacket."

I settled myself at Jean's head, somehow managing to get into a position so I could cradle her head in my lap with both of us perched on the rocks. We struggled to get her into the down jacket. As Jay zipped it I noticed her feet. The rubber sandals were missing now, and her feet were white and naked and seemed horribly vulnerable. I unzipped my boots, stripped off my warm blue socks, and worked them onto her feet. They came to her calf.

It's all I can do for you, Jean, I thought. She was as warm as we could make her. I looked at the bright blue socks and thought of the Earth Shoe store in Berkeley. It seemed light-years away now. I put my boots back on, trying not to notice how thin the leather was or how cold and sticky the paper innersoles felt against my bare feet.

Then I looked at Jean more closely and saw that her hair was matted with blood and that blood clogged her mouth and nose. "Should I try to clean out her nose so she can breathe?" I asked Jay.

"No," he answered. "Her air passages are clear."

He must have checked her already, I thought. *He's seen enough injured animals to know.*

I cleared the hair off Jean's face, separating the strands. That was when I saw the cuts: three deep, terrible slits on her left cheek, slashes that radiated from her mouth to her ear, precise ravines that seem stamped into her face. I thought about how she would look when this was all over. Her face was going to be a mass of stitches. Almost certainly she would have to have plastic surgery. I examined her face. She was wearing no makeup and looked so very young and innocent, but the prettiness was scarred now. I thought: *She will never look the same again, not ever*.

"Jean," Jay called sharply. "Jean, can you hear me?" I could tell that speaking was an effort for him. He was having trouble getting his breath too, but he continued calling.

Jean's body shuddered. She was moving, as if to try to find a resting place on these obstinate rocks. But there was no comfortable place. We sat there for a long time like that. Now and then Jay would double over and moan.

"My gut hurts something fierce," he said. "I think the seatbelt gouged me."

I knew what he meant. My body was paining now too. If I let my mind focus on any of the assorted cuts, the pain increased, so I determined to ignore them as much as I could. Breathing was an effort, moving was an effort, conversation was an effort. We limited movement as much as we could and spoke only when we had to, along the way dropping all the unnecessary words or phrases.

"The air is thin up here," Jay explained, "but we should get used to it in a while."

A while. Time. I realized I had lost all sense of time. Jay looked at his watch as if he too had just thought about it. The crystal was broken.

"It stopped at 2:15," he said. "That must have been when we hit." His tone was flat; it was as if the time was not important, just another extraneous issue that could be ignored.

"If you can move your fingers does it mean your arm isn't broken?" I asked.

I could see that Jay was trying to sort out the question. At first he looked at me as though I were talking about something totally out of context, something insignificant. "No," he answered, "not necessarily." He didn't ask why I wanted to know and I didn't offer to tell him. But I stored away the information: My arm was broken.

Jean opened her eyes and groaned, and Jay moved to her.

"Lie still," I said as loud as I could, hoping to make contact. But there was no contact. Jean began to move, to moan in soft tones that would rise and fall, becoming anguished and then pleading.

"Please, Jean, try to be still," I begged, alarmed at the power of her movements. She could not hear me. I understood that, but I couldn't totally accept it.

"Jean, please try to be quiet," I pleaded, not knowing what else to do. I could see no cuts on her body; she seemed all right but she wasn't coming around. Her body was moving in jerking, spastic convulsions. Broken beer bottles from the plane lay all around us, and some with jagged bottoms were threateningly close to Jean. I crawled over to pick up those in her path and flung them down the slope. I could hear the sound of the glass splintering far below us.

"We've got to get her back into the plane," I said to Jay. "If you can get her feet I'll manage her arms." It was the first decision I had made. Jay acquiesced.

We tried. I held her under the arms and pulled her a few inches while Jay attempted to lift her feet. We struggled with her for a few minutes, then crumpled in a heap in the rocks. Jay and I gasped for breath, exhausted from the attempt. We could not even lift her, much less move her back into the plane.

"I just—can't," Jay said finally. He did not look at me. He was bent over, his arms tight over his stomach.

"Look," I said, "you try to radio for help while I hold on to Jean so she doesn't fall any farther." It was an admission of defeat. We would have to count on somebody else helping Jean, helping us all. And quickly. They must come quickly.

By now Jean had edged dangerously down the steep slope. The upper part of her body would wrench violently, sending her hurtling from the boulder she was on to the one below it.

I held on to her as hard as I could, afraid that she would pull us both down the slope yet afraid to let go. I clutched the straps of her overalls and dug my feet into the rocks for leverage. I prayed that she would stay still, that I would not have to watch her body make those lunatic lunges. I turned away from her and watched Jay struggle to get back to the plane. Already Jean had taken us a distance down the slope. It was a long time before I heard him talking into the radio.

"Mayday! Mayday! Anyone can you read me?" There was a tremor in his voice that I had not heard before, and that I did not want to hear. "Mayday! Mayday! This is Cessna N52855. We're down on the Sierra crest at Kearsarge Pass, six to eight miles north of Mt. Whitney. Anyone! Please!"

We waited, in the crystal quiet, for an answer—the crackle of the radio, a voice, a sound. We waited until there was no more reason to wait. I could hear him click the battery off, and I knew he had not been able to get a message through.

It seemed like hours before Jay reached us again. I tried to forget the rising fear I had heard in his voice. I told myself we would have to try later, that we should not give up on the radio altogether.

Jean began to pull more strongly now. She was struggling against me and I wanted to switch arms but I couldn't. I had to favor my left arm now, had to hold it in reserve. My fingers grew numb but I kept them twisted around her overall straps. I tried to shut my ears to the noises she was making. I knew I would always remember them with an agonizing vividness, the way I remembered the noises that came from my neighbor's back yard when she was butchering rabbits. I was very young then, and I watched her, not knowing what was happening. I was morbidly fascinated in the way that children sometimes are, and frightened by it too. The rabbits made a sound—sharp, futile, anguished. An animal sound, a kind of bleating.

Jay reached out and grabbed Jean, realizing that it would take both of us to hold her. The upper part of her body flopped forward and down.

"We have to radio again," I insisted. "We have to keep trying."

Without looking at me, Jay said slowly, "I've activated an emergency radio beacon in the tail section of the plane. It's got its own power source. It'll keep sending signals to help a search party find us, even without a sighting."

A search party. Of course! Someone would come looking for us—but when?

"But we'll keep trying the radio too?" I asked.

Jay didn't answer.

This time I wasn't going to let him off. "Jay, we've got to keep trying."

"Go ahead if you want to," he said.

"But I don't know how. You know how; you have to do it."

I waited, but again he didn't answer. He just sat there, hanging on to Jean, not saying anything.

"Okay, then," I said finally, "I'll do it. But you've got to tell me exactly what to do. Every move, everything."

"Well, you turn on the battery. There's a switch."

I took a deep breath and tried to get specific directions from him. When I had some idea of what to do, I headed toward the plane. The climb back did not seem quite so steep this time. The sun was warm on my back as I ducked under the wing and into the cockpit. I was concentrating so hard on what Jay had told me that I didn't hear him until he came in and took over from me.

In the time since the crash we had been preoccupied with Jean. When he joined me at the radio, he did not mention her, and neither did I. Instead I asked, "Will there be a search party?"

He told me what I must already have known. "Not this afternoon, for sure." It was a fact, an obvious fact.

When Jay didn't elaborate, I started to demand details. "When is your daughter expecting you back?" I tried my best to remember his daughter's name and couldn't.

"Carla?" he answered, as if bringing her up was a novel idea. "Carla gets home from school about three, but she probably won't start to wonder where I am until around dinner time. I don't always get home before six."

The sun was still high, so I figured it was no more than midafternoon, probably about three o'clock. Carla might be home right now. I tried to think what a little girl would be doing, alone in the house—maybe lying on a bed, reading. Not alarmed, not yet. Probably not for another three hours or more.

"Does Carla know where you were going?" I probed, not willing to let go.

"I don't know," he answered. "I'm not sure. I think I might have left the name of the woman in Furnace Creek on a scrap of paper on the desk. Maybe she'll find it."

Good Lord. He wasn't sure if his ten-year-old daughter knew he was going flying today. Didn't he make any contingency plans for her? It all seemed so haphazard, so slipshod. *No flight plan. Nobody knows where we are. I don't even know where we are,* I thought. There was nobody to sound the alarm.

It hit me then: *I am on my own.* Jay couldn't take care of me and I couldn't expect him to. We were in this together. We could help each other but there had to be a balance.

"Jimmie expects me back about six," I said out loud. "I'm not sure how long it'll be before he gets alarmed, or what he will do. Please, Jimmie, send somebody looking for us!"

My outburst didn't seem to faze Jay. Like Jean, he was

51

working to find some comfortable niche in the rocks. He wanted to stretch out, which struck me as strange, since my instinct was the opposite. I wanted to curl up in as tight a knot as possible, keeping my fingers tucked under my armpits and my toes under my skirt.

Below us to the west was a basin covered with snow, and a bit farther down was the first line of trees. There would be more space there, I figured, and perhaps the trees would offer some protection. "Do you think we should try to get down to the trees?" I asked.

This time Jay didn't hesitate. "No," he said, "we should stay with the aircraft." I didn't argue; obviously, he knew the proper procedure. There was probably a rule about it: *Chance of survival is greater if you stay with the downed craft.* Even if the craft is stuck on the top of one of the highest mountains on the continent. Even if you can't stand up straight and nobody misses you yet.

"Have you ever been in a plane crash before?" I blurted.

Jay looked at me as if I had taken leave of my senses. He snorted and did not answer. He just sat there shaking his head, and I thought that he must be chastising himself.

"I did a dumb thing," he said finally, "really dumb." He bent over and hugged his knees. He groaned but he didn't cry. We were both beyond tears. I felt a surge of sorrow for him.

"Look, Jay," I said, as softly as I could, "it's done. I don't know if it helps any, but I'm not angry. I don't blame you." I didn't finish my thought. I didn't tell him I wasn't angry because it wouldn't do any good; it would be a waste of energy, and we were going to need all the energy we could muster. We were going to have to think this whole thing out, together. We would have to pool our resources. We needed each other.

We needed a plan, I knew that. "I'm climbing to the top, to the crest," I told Jay. I thought that this is what you do when you are lost: You seek the highest point to see what you can see. Reconnoiter. Scout. I had never been lost in the mountains before, but I had rambled all over the countryside on horseback and I had hiked the trails in enough national parks to know how to read a pathway. I told myself: *If you remember to keep your head you will find a way out. If you do not panic.*

For a time after the crash I had been numb, but now my body was beginning to complain. I could feel a stiffness in my right leg; the thigh had ballooned just above the knee and it made climbing difficult. My tongue hurt like crazy, so I grabbed one of the beer bottles that had somehow survived the crash intact, twisted off the cap, and took a long drink. It was icy cold but soothing to my bleeding mouth. A nagging pain throbbed in my left forearm, and I decided to stuff my hand into my jacket pocket. I let the arm dangle there, saving it for later. Something was very wrong with it, but it was going to have to work for me. That's all there was to it.

I worked my way up the mountain, covering the fifteen feet in a new, steady pace. On the crest, lapping over from the eastern side of the mountains, were some hard patches of snow. I stood when I finally reached the top, and a cold updraft billowed up my skirt and hit my exposed flesh. I hardly noticed. What I saw overwhelmed me.

My God in heaven. I gasped.

Below me, just below my toes, was an almost vertical drop, thousands and thousands of feet, a dizzying plunge to the desert floor below.

Nearly straight down. On the eastern side of the Sierras there were no forests, no layers of mountains, no mile-upon-mile of wilderness. No real impediments at all. Just right—down—there. I felt that I could reach out and touch the valley below us.

I wanted to shriek for joy. *Hey, everybody, we're not lost after all. Look, right down there: people, settlements, houses, ranches. There's a whole valley down there.* I thought I could make out an airstrip. *Hey, everybody, we are not lost and I can do something. I can go for help.*

Jay's voice carried up to me. "Mayday, Mayday." He was droning into the radio. There was no quiver or panic in his voice now. I called out to him to join me. For a minute I thought he wasn't going to make the effort, but then he seemed to change his mind and began to lumber up the steep slope. I wondered if I was moving with the same kind of thickness. Finally Jay heaved himself next to me and we stood together, saying nothing, looking to the east.

"Is that Owens Valley down there?" I asked.

When he nodded I thought my heart would burst.

I knew Owens Valley! I had been through that very valley three years before at just about this time of year. I remembered the drive perfectly, remembered watching these very peaks from below. The mountains had not seemed real to me then; viewed from below they were breathtaking, beyond belief. I knew there were people down there—towns and roads and ranches and help. We weren't in the middle of nowhere after all; we were on the far side of the Sierras. We could even see across the valley to another range of mountains, stark, lower-lying mountains the color of terra cotta.

"How long would it take me to hike down?" I asked.

Jay shrugged.

The days were long. It would be light for another three, maybe four hours. Probably I wouldn't even have to go all the way down before I came upon a ranch. There would be roads in the mountains, of course. There were roads everywhere these days. *Nothing is as it seems, not ever,* I thought.

My excitement was mounting. I could do something. I could go for help and they would bring a helicopter up here and get Jay and put Jean on a stretcher and everything would turn out all right.

"Jay, it looks so close. I'm going to try to hike out."

For a minute he didn't say anything and didn't look at me. Then, in the same noncommittal tone he had used since the crash, he said, "Go ahead. Just head straight down for the desert."

I looked at him for a long moment but couldn't see any expression under the crust of blood that covered his face. His hands were in his pockets and he was hunched forward, his shoulders drawn high. "What about you?" I asked, not really knowing what I meant by the question, but needing to know what plans he had, if any. When he didn't answer I said, "If a search party gets here today you can tell them which way I went."

He didn't bother to respond. We both knew there wouldn't be a search party, not that day.

I rummaged through the back of the plane for my backpack and carefully selected the things I thought might come in handy: a fruit knife, a tangerine and a sandwich, a map that looked as if it might be useful, my camera and billfold. I had begun to think of civilization again. I would need identification and money. And I didn't want to lose my valuable camera.

"I'm going," I said to Jay. "I'll try to hurry."

He said, "Okay." Nothing more.

I figured there was plenty of time to make it to the desert before dark. The route seemed very direct. For a while I moved back and forth along the crest, looking for just the right place to start my descent. The beginning would be in snow. I tested the snow at my feet. The sun had softened it, but there was still a hard crust of ice on the top. That crust should hold me. I could see now that the steepest part of the climb down was at the very top; it was like a tea cup, almost vertical at the rim and rounding off into a bowl below. The trick was to get down to the easier slopes in the bowl.

Finally I decided on a spot, crouched, and carefully lowered myself over the side. I kicked a toehold in the ice with

55

one boot, then with the other. I punched holes in the ice with my fists. The ice crust would have to hold me, I realized. The rocks were buried beneath the snow.

The snow was a blinding white, the sky a shade of blue that does not exist at lower altitudes—an intense, painful blue. I kicked in another two holes, then two more. I was moving down the face of this mountain, one notch at a time. My left arm was doing its work. It hadn't caved in on me. Punch, kick, punch, kick.

When I had gone perhaps six feet over the side I tilted my head back to view my progress. I realized immediately that I had made a terrible mistake. The sky began to spin, to turn and turn, faster and faster. The snow crust under my hand began to give way, and suddenly my body seemed weak beyond belief.

All I could think was: *Sweet Jesus, it didn't look anywhere near this steep from above.* I could fall, here and now, go spinning down into the bowl below with nothing to break my fall for hundreds of feet. One little slip and I would be lost. For an instant I felt impaled, trapped, able to go neither up nor down.

No, I told myself. Just that: *No.* I took a deep breath and slowly, slowly, began to pull myself back up. I used the same holes, praying the ice would hold. As if in answer, a chunk came off in my hand. I let go of it and grabbed a small ice ledge. I didn't feel the cold, didn't feel the ice in my hands or the cold drafts blowing up my skirt. All I felt was the need to get back up. *Don't panic,* I told myself over and over again. *Slow down, go slow, slow.*

I scrambled over the top and lay there, drained of all energy. I had miscalculated. Disappointment replaced the excitement of only a few minutes before. But I felt a certain relief too. I knew I had made a mistake, but it had not been fatal. The sun was still warm; there was still a chance.

After a bit I got up and started the climb down to the

plane. I could see Jay in the same position I had left him, leaning against a door that had fallen off the plane, watching me indifferently.

Jean was no longer in sight.

6

Jay was looking at me, I could see that, but he was fading in and fading out. His face was clear one moment and a blur the next. A foggy blackness began to move in on the periphery of my sight, closing in like a camera lens until I seemed to be looking through a small, round hole. A hush moved into my ears.

I was going to pass out.

I sat down, dropped my head between my knees, and screamed silently to myself: *Don't let go.* I had to hold on to consciousness, I knew it. I had to will myself to stay awake or I would die. *You are okay okay okay.* The words echoed in the far reaches of my mind. *Hang on, don't let go.* Slowly the spinning stopped and my peripheral vision returned. I was exhausted from the effort to climb down. I had overestimated my strength.

I sat there, my head dangling between my legs, in a kind

of twilight zone. From that upside-down position I caught a glimpse of what was left of my glasses. The lenses were shattered and the gold metal frames were twisted out of shape. I noticed they were spattered with blood. My hands flew to my face. Could I be slashed too? My bruised, numb fingers searched but could find no open wounds. I said a small prayer of thanks.

The most astounding thing about finding the glasses was that I had not noticed they were gone. Without them my whole perception changes, yet until that moment I had not missed them. I had looked at the valley below, envisioned it so close, and I hadn't been wearing my glasses.

We had been on this solid slab of granite for well over an hour and I was still making miraculous discoveries. I wondered if there was something I should be doing that I hadn't thought of. *Think, Lauren, think,* I said to myself. *Breathe in and breathe out, breathe deeply and think straight.* That was it; the first thing to do was get calm. If I was going to do battle on this mountaintop I would have to keep my balance in every way.

I noticed the little pot that had held the desert plant Jay was taking to the woman in Furnace Creek. The pot was cracked open and the plant was upside down, its roots exposed. I looked at the gift for a long time; I had never seen anything that seemed so poignant, so desperately out of place.

Then something peculiar happened: I got angry. It came simmering up from inside. I thought: *That's not going to happen to me. I am going to get down from here. That's not going to happen to me.*

Anger displaced inertia and I began to pick my way back to Jay. He was standing, his shoulders hunched and his hands in his pockets, still looking at me in a distracted way, as if I were someone he knew once, long ago, but whose name he had forgotten.

59

"I couldn't make it," I managed to say. "It was just too steep."

He shrugged. It didn't seem to matter to him one way or the other.

There was no breeze and the sun was surprisingly warm. The air, although cold at that high altitude, was reasonably comfortable. As long as we kept still it didn't seem to hurt to breathe, and at times we were lulled into a kind of pleasant stupor. We stayed like that for a long time, saying nothing. I wanted to ask some questions but I didn't. It was like being on a bus full of strangers. You want to ask another passenger directions but he seems absorbed in himself. He is civil to you, no more. Gradually the nagging inside of you—the need to know—builds until you work up the courage to speak.

I wanted to say, "Listen, Jay, you're supposed to know what to do in an emergency. You're the one everybody says is so terrific in a crisis. So okay, Jay, this is a crisis. Do something! Be terrific! Work with me." In the end I said nothing because I realized it wouldn't help.

Saving ourselves. That was what it was all about. We couldn't just sit in the sun, doing nothing. Because the sun was going to go down. *And it must follow as the night the day*—the line was embedded in my memory, left over from some English literature course. The sun was moving west, and I knew it would sink into the Pacific in another hour or so. I could see my mother sitting in her cane-backed chair by the French doors, watching the sun fall into the ocean. I was glad she didn't know where I was or what was happening up here, glad that it would all be over before she even knew I was gone. Then we could sit around and talk about it and I could tell my parents what happened. I wondered how Jay would describe the accident then.

"It was so damned dumb," he said again, as if in answer to my unspoken question. The words tumbled out, and I sensed an underlying anguish.

60

"What did happen?" I asked for the first time. "Why didn't we make it over the crest?"

He shook his head and rubbed a fist into his eyes. "I should have circled, should have made another approach to gain altitude. There were downdrafts." He dropped his head and moaned.

I could not think of what to say. Instead, I leaned over and pulled up the nylon hood of his windbreaker so that it covered his head. He let me tie it. "Better keep as warm as possible," I said.

I thought of Jean. Was there any chance of finding her, of sheltering her somehow? Jay could never help, and without him I'd have no chance. Even if I could find her—and I dreaded the thought of making another descent—I had nothing with which to shelter her. And I knew I could not possibly move her myself.

The trees were far below us and were rooted in deep snow. Winter was everywhere. The sun and the warmth of this day could be no more than the briefest hiatus. Clouds could roll in on us at any time. What you expect on a mountaintop are cold-blowing winds and subzero temperatures.

I wanted to warn Jay. From the moment we crashed I wanted to feel close to him, to know that we were in this together. If there were two of us, I reasoned, we would have a better chance to make it. I couldn't understand how Jay could fail to see that. If I had known him better, I felt, I would have understood why he was creating the distance between us. Was he crumpled with self-loathing because he felt responsible? Was he tormented by the thought of Jean, beyond our view, injured and alone? Or was it self-pity because his stomach hurt? I didn't know.

"It's cold enough for a fire," I said. "We need matches and we need something to burn." I crawled into the plane— hard work, since it rested at something like a fifty-degree angle on the steep slope. My purse was lying on the floor. I rummaged through it, praying for one of the folders of matches I usually keep there for friends who smoke. I handed Jean's purse out to Jay for him to go through. We searched everywhere and came up blank.

"Doesn't this plane have first-aid or emergency supplies or something?" I was surprised to hear annoyance in my voice.

"The cigarette lighter," Jay answered.

"Thank God for smokers!" I said for the first time in my life. We collected everything that we thought would burn, sparing only the plane's log. (I stood holding it, thinking that there would be an investigation, that the log would be important; then I tucked it back into the plane in a safe place.) I took out the maps, the paper sack that held our lunch, and the wooden cat cage, and I removed the beer from the cardboard cartons.

"We should probably eat something," I suggested when I came upon the lunch. I hadn't thought of food all day and I wasn't hungry now, but it seemed like something we should do. I handed Jay a sandwich and bit into a peanut butter and jelly. It was a mistake; my mouth was sore and the sandwich was full of gravel. I couldn't swallow so I spat it out.

Food was not on Jay's mind either. "Let's get a fire going," he said. "Try to find more things to burn." I was surprised that he expected me to do the moving, the collecting. "See if you can get the seats out," he directed. "They'd burn a long time."

I tried to pry the front seats loose, but they were wedged in tight. I took the fruit knife and tried to slash the seats open in order to get at the stuffing. But the knife was too dull, and I couldn't even manage a slit. Systematically, we considered which parts of the plane would burn. We thought about trying to remove the tires, but they had collapsed under the plane and were beyond our reach. Other than the seats there was nothing.

62

"How cold do you think it is now?" I asked, my teeth chattering.

"Maybe twenty-eight or thirty degrees," Jay answered. "When the sun is out and there isn't any wind it seems warmer than it actually is at this altitude."

At least that is what he tried to say, but the words came out scrambled. Mine did too. I could hear myself say, "The fire—do you think—start it we might—now?" The thoughts were in order in my head, but they just wouldn't come out straight. It baffled me. The impact had cracked my teeth. Could it have cracked my brain too? Was I brain-damaged? But Jay was doing it too. If it wasn't brain damage, what could it be?

Shock. I fixed on the word. That was it, we must be in shock. The explanation satisfied me completely and I dismissed it from my mind. It didn't matter that I had no clear idea what shock was. I knew it happened to people who had been in accidents. I figured it would wear off.

We piled our small store of combustibles near the plane. I twisted a piece of brown bag into a tight stick to use as a torch between the cigarette lighter and the fire. It was going to be tricky, I knew.

"You do it," Jay said, just as I was about to ask him to take on the firemaking chore.

"I don't know if I can." I started to protest.

"You can," he said, and it was decided.

I climbed back in, took a deep breath, switched on the battery, and felt a leap of hope at the whirring sound it made. *Work, please work,* I prayed under my breath. I pushed the lighter in hard. After a long, suspenseful pause it popped out again.

"Hooray!" I whooped when I saw the glowing orange circles. I stuck the piece of paper into them and waited for it to catch.

"Blow on it," Jay said from outside.

I blew. Nothing happened. A small cone of black appeared on the paper and smoked, nothing else.

"Blow harder," he said. "Cup your hand and blow."

I did. Nothing.

"Jay, you try," I pleaded. "You're better at this kind of thing."

"I can't," he told me. "It hurts too much to bend over."

It hurts too much! My God, didn't he think I hurt too? Didn't he know that hurting didn't count, that getting the fire going was all that counted? Especially when there was something peculiar about fire up here.

"I'll douse the punk in gasoline," Jay said. "That should make it flame." He took the twist of paper, dipped it in a puddle of gasoline, and gave it back to me.

Anything, I thought, *I'll try anything.* It would probably explode in my hands, but I didn't care. All I wanted was a flame.

The gas fumes filled the cockpit and made me choke. Sputtering, I pushed the cigarette lighter in again, praying it would still work. It did. This time the paper burst into flame.

I cheered as I passed it to Jay. At the same time, I was afraid it would go out before he could get to our pile of paper and wood. I held my breath as he crouched. I could see the flames lick up and seem to vanish in the air. The fire was elusive, like something a magician might conjure up: I couldn't tell if it was real or not and I didn't know when it would vanish altogether.

Oxygen. Of course! Fire needs oxygen to burn, humans need oxygen to breathe, and there just wasn't enough oxygen up there. I knew there was an equation, if only I could figure it out: Oxygen is to survival as fire is to—what? Or oxygen is to fire as fire is to—what?

The small pile of wood and paper ignited, and Jay sank back against the padded door that had fallen off the plane.

The plastic padding gave him a small space to stretch out. I perched on a flat boulder close by, bunched up as small as I could make myself, soaking in the warmth that the small fire was giving off. I buried my nose in my blouse just to breathe in the warmth of my own body.

It was nice. We relaxed, faces and hands pressed as close to the fire as we could get them. Jay's tennis shoes were almost into the fire. I wished I were wearing a big down jacket—and underpants, especially underpants, so the cold gusts of air didn't torment my exposed ass. I wished I were all curled up in a blanket, warm and cozy, my toes nice and toasted.

"Jay, keep your hands in your pockets," I snapped, pulling myself back to reality. He grunted a "mind your own business" kind of grunt which erased the safe feeling the fire had given me. It was going out, fast.

"Throw some gas on it," Jay said.

"Why?" I asked. "There's nothing left to burn, so why throw gas?"

"Because the gas will burn. Just throw it on the rocks and it will give off a lot of heat."

"We'll need some containers, something to catch it in," I said, picking up a beer bottle that was sitting nearby and starting to empty it.

"Wait, wait." Jay stopped me. "Pass that here." He drained it and gave it back to me.

I crawled under the wing and began to fill the bottle from the leaking spigot attached to one of the plane's gas tanks. "No," I wailed, "it's been leaking all afternoon. We've wasted so much, I wonder if there's enough left."

"Plenty left," Jay muttered.

This time I was not reassured. I wanted to believe him but I didn't, quite.

Over my shoulder I could see that the fire was getting low. I moved back, poured on the gasoline, and was relieved to see it flame high. But I needed more containers; I had no reserve bottle of gas. Jay was twisting open another beer, but there wasn't enough time. The fire went out before we could figure out a system.

I crawled around the plane, looking for intact bottles. I collected three. Then I crawled back to Jay and helped myself to a bottle of beer.

"We'd better drink as much as we can," Jay sputtered between gulps. It's all the liquid we've got—dehydration."

I understood. As I tilted my head back to finish a bottle, something slushed forward. I touched it with my tongue. Ice! The beer had started to freeze and the sun was still up. It was so cold already that alcoholic beverages would freeze. Good God. We were going to need every bottle we could get. I gathered ten in all, then squatted under the wing and lodged one bottle against the crook of the gas spigot. When it was full, I immediately switched to another, then took the full bottle back to Jay.

The sun was casting long shadows, deep blue indentations in the mountains that lay below us. The colors were piercingly clear. I sat, transfixed, watching the sun glow into the purest, deepest vermilion. It seemed to permeate everything, flowing over us in waves, washing us in a shimmer of radiance.

"I've never seen anything like this before," I said, "never, not in all my life." For a long minute we stood together, bathed in the delicate light.

"It's going to get cold now, really cold—and fast," Jay said.

Even as he spoke I could feel the air grow cooler. I went back to the plane with a piece of paper we had saved from the first fire. The gas-soaked torch flared up, and this time I was glad. I threw it out on the rocks, picked up a bottle of gas and splashed it on the flames. There was a sputtering and a cloud of black smoke.

"Too much, too much," Jay cautioned. "Try to shoot out a steady stream of gas, shoot it evenly."

I tried again. This time there was a whoosh and a burst of light as the fire leaped to the sky.

"You do it," I said to Jay, handing him a bottle and crawling back under the wing to line up the next bottle to be filled. I was determined not to waste another drop of gas now that I knew how important it was.

I counted the steps, using my good right arm to steady myself on the boulders, being careful to avoid those I knew to be loose. My slip had ridden up, and the cut between my legs was bleeding now and then, making the skirt mat to my skin. I kept pulling it loose so that I could move, and then the cold air would blossom up and under. It was a miserable sensation. I felt even more miserable when I saw the bottle was full and spilling over.

"Jay," I shouted, "you've got to help me. It's going to take two of us to keep these bottles rotating so we don't lose any gas, and I just can't handle it alone."

"Let it run over" was his answer. "There's plenty."

What he was saying, I realized with a sinking feeling, was that he didn't plan to take a turn, that if the bottles were going to get filled at all it would be up to me to do it. Damn! I wanted to shake him, to wake him up. I wanted him to take on some responsibility. Or maybe I just didn't want to accept the role he was forcing on me. *We were both intact,* and that should have made us equal, but it didn't.

I crawled back to where he was sitting, propped against the door in the same position I had left him, and I handed him a bottle. Then I had to crawl back over him to throw my own gas. If I tried to do it on the other side, closer to the spigot, I risked splashing Jay and setting him on fire.

"Could you at least move?" I snapped. "This way I have to climb over you every time I go for gas." My aggravation was mounting. "Damn it, Jay, we're in this together and

67

you've got to do your share. I can't do it all by myself." I could hear the petulance in my voice and didn't like it, but I couldn't seem to help it either. At any rate, it had no effect on Jay. If he heard me he gave no sign.

So the routine was set. I had a line of bottles waiting under the plane, the last one spilling over before we could burn the full bottles. I would take one for me and one for Jay and, crawling over him, go back to take my turn sending a steady stream into the rocks, to be rewarded with flames that threw off a wonderful heat.

Darkness had moved up from the valleys. We might have been on a dead planet out in space, the cold and the dark were that complete. There was no moon; the only light came from the fire. I could not imagine being without that light and that heat. The cold to our backs was bitter.

Jay's aim was much better than mine. He seemed to have more control of the gasoline. He could throw a stream into the fire, then let the flames get low before spurting a new stream into them. Sometimes he waited so long that I became alarmed and called to him; but always, at what seemed the last possible moment, he would send a jet of gas and it would flare up again.

The fire was capricious. After a while I learned that I could sit back and rest for five minutes or so before returning for another bottle. I focused on those minutes, concentrated on them when I began to feel weary, so that I could gather the energy to make another trip. I would sit as close to Jay as I could, feeling the heat of my face and the cold behind me, and I would think: *One more trip, then another and another.* And then I would say to myself: *Think only of the next one, no more.*

Once Jay said, "Poor Jean."

"What was Jean's last name?" I remembered to ask. It had been important to me that morning.

"Noller," Jay answered. "Her name was Noller." *Was.* He used the past tense too.

"She can't survive out there, not in this cold." I put our fear into words.

"No," he answered.

Jean was dead. She had to be. It was a fact, like the cold to our backs—a cruel fact that we held off, away from us. I don't know when I knew she was dead, or when Jay knew. We talked about it in thin, brief phrases, facing the fire, the elusive, fragile fire that stood between us and the cold and the kind of death that had already overtaken Jean.

I was sitting slightly higher than Jay. I wanted us to share the warmth of being alive, together. I reached down and held his hand in mine. It was surprisingly cold, so I began to rub it. Then I leaned over and kissed him on the top of his head. I caressed him and stroked his hair.

"I'm not angry with you, Jay," I said again, as low and as straight as I could. I noticed my voice was quivering. "I really want you to know that—it's important. I don't blame you. All I want is for us to get out of this together; I want to get through this night." I needed to make contact with him because he was alive and I was alive. I wanted to hear him say, "Yes, we're going to make it together."

"Please, Jay, can we make a pact, an agreement?" I asked. "Can we promise that we'll see each other through the night, that we'll make it together?" I wanted it so badly, that pact; it seemed that everything depended on it. "Promise, Jay?" I pleaded.

"Yes," he said. "Sure, we'll make it."

I felt a lot better then. "Put your hands in your pockets," I said before I got up to pull yet another bottle out and replace it with an empty.

I wasn't sure how many trips I had made—thirty, maybe more. The bottles kept filling faster than we could empty them, and there was nothing to do about it except try to keep alert. The *do nots* had become a litany: Do not slip and fall, do not get sloppy with the gasoline, do not get drowsy.

Once I splashed the gas out of the bottle and onto my hand, and before I knew what was happening the fire had worked its way up to the bottle. I stood there for a long moment before I reacted to Jay's yell.

"Throw it!" he said. "Fast!"

I flung the flaming bottle away from me, and it exploded against the rocks in a wild burst.

"My God!" I gasped. "That's what a Molotov cocktail is."

"It could have blown your hand off," Jay admonished.

"But we've forfeited a bottle," I wailed, angry at what my carelessness had cost us.

"Better the bottle than your hand," he came back, and I would have been comforted by his concern had I not been so shaken. He finally seemed to care about what happened to us.

I was coming apart then. Fatigue had saturated my body. Inside of me, in that part that was important to keep still, everything was moving, every molecule bumping into every other. I needed to sort them out, to get them quiet again.

A mantra might work. *Om mani peme hum hri,* I began softly, under my breath the way I had been taught at the Tibetan Institute. *Om mani peme hum hri.* I wanted to empty my mind, let the sound calm me down. *Om mani peme hum hri.* I could feel the vibration beginning to build.

"What's that? What are you doing?" Jay howled, obviously disconcerted.

"It's a mantra," I explained, thinking that maybe if I told him about it, about how I happened to go to the Tibetan Institute, he wouldn't be so put off by my humming. "I signed up for this training program last year. It was meditation and relaxation techniques, a program for mental health professionals. At the time, I was working at a halfway house for young adults, kids who had just been released from county mental facilities. It was an eight-week course that taught some basic meditation techniques." I could hear myself rattling on, jabbering away, but I couldn't seem to stop. "The funny thing about it was that it was full of Ph.D. candidates from all over the place—New York, Holland, Germany—a kind of international medley of people."

Jay wanted none of it. "Just cut it out," he snapped. "That's all."

But it wasn't all; I wasn't going to let it be all. I was testy now, determined to draw him into something that would keep us going. "Okay, then," I said, "let's talk. Tell me some cowboy stories. Tell me about when you were on the ranch."

He stared into the fire for a long while, and when he finally spoke his voice was low and husky. "No," he said. "No cowboy stories, not now."

Something in his voice made me drop it. I took a new tack. "Then let's sing," I insisted. "Sing with me. C'mon."

I started in a quavering voice: "Oh, Mary, don't you weep don't you mourn, Pharaoh's army got drownded."

Terrific, I thought sarcastically. *That's all we need right now, a song about death.*

I started over again. "Swing low, sweet chariot, Comin' for to carry me home." I broke off in a wail. What rotten taste. Didn't I know any songs that weren't funereal?

Then I thought of good old Pete Seeger, whose songs I had sung at peace rallys. "Kum-ba-ya, my Lord, kum-ba-ya." I sang the lullaby all the way through, soothed by the sounds as I had been by the mantra. This time Jay did not object, although he did not join in. I sang as I got up to make my way over Jay, then over the rocks to the bottle and back again. "Hush, little baby, don't you cry, Mama's gonna get you a butterfly." I sang them all, over and over again. I sang them at the top of this granite mountain, raising my voice in the wilderness, burning my small candle in the dark.

As I made the trips back and forth, I became obsessed with the notion that we were poisoning ourselves. Sometimes the fumes seemed to choke me, and I thought that our lungs were turning black inside, the way the fuselage of the plane was becoming coated with oily, black soot.

"Could it kill us?" I asked Jay, the medical expert.

He didn't answer, and it no longer struck me as strange that he didn't. Instead, I moved as far away from the fire as I could bear and took a deep breath of unadulterated air. The cold came rushing in, cutting down into my lungs like a surgical knife, reminding me that no matter how harmful the gas fumes were, the cold was worse by far.

"Hurry," Jay called to me once, as I went for a new bottle of gas. I knew it had to be important for him to call out like that. I could see from under the wing that the fire was perilously low. *It's going out,* I said to myself. But I didn't have time to get back. There was nothing to do but aim a spurt of gas from where I was standing.

The gas splashed on Jay and in an instant he was aflame.

"Oh, God, Jay, I'm so sorry," I said. He waved me away with his hand.

"It's okay. Go back for the bottle," he directed.

At least, I thought, *it's good that the fire is easily snuffed out. At least we won't immolate ourselves.*

The fire would wander among the rocks, working its way down the hill and then back up again as if it had a life and will of its own. Now and then it would flare in some unexpected spot—a place we had sprayed with gas that had not yet ignited. Sometimes I would pour on too much and send a great tower of light into the sky so we could see each other clearly. It would send choking clouds of smoke boiling at us.

But it would also illuminate Jay's face, with its mask of dark dried blood. It was primitive and grotesque, and I reached over to try to rub it off—a fragile effort to set things straight again.

"Don't touch me," he said peevishly. "Leave it alone."

After that we didn't speak for maybe an hour. I wasn't angry or anything; it was just that the night was dragging so interminably. Once I heard a droning that became louder and louder; finally I realized that it was a jet, probably an airliner headed for San Francisco. *People on their way home. They'll be there in half an hour.* The thought was stunning. Excited, I poured a great stream of gas onto the fire and sent a spiral of flame high into the blackness.

"Don't bother," Jay said.

"Why not?" I wanted to know. "Why not?"

"It won't help," he answered calmly. "They can't see you."

I was defiant. "They *might* see us," I said. "They might report it and somebody would come to put it out. It is possible, it is!" I was practically shouting.

"No," he answered evenly, "they won't see it and they won't come, not tonight."

I started back for the next bottle, not wanting to go but knowing I would, putting my body on automatic controls and ignoring the cuts and hurts and aches. I came back with two bottles and handed one to Jay. He took it without a word. We continued as we had for what seemed like forever. *Night without end, amen.* I wanted to quit but I couldn't; there simply was no other option. The only way I could get off the mountain was to feed the fire. The fire was synonymous with survival; without it we could not survive. I was the firetender, the one who had to keep it going throughout the long night. I thought about how there had always been firetenders. They had kept civilization's night fires since the beginning. I was but one in a long line of firetenders.

"My gut aches something fierce," Jay said for the third or fourth time. He was slurring his words a bit; and though I tried not to hear it, an edge of complaint—a hint of a whine—had crept into his voice.

I wanted to say, "Can it." I felt like being crude, even mean. I wanted to tell him that I didn't want to hear about how much he hurt because it was all I could do to manage my own throbbing body. I wanted to say that the complaint department was closed. I said nothing.

Whether it was out of fatigue or out of pique I don't know, but suddenly I splattered some gas on my face. I dropped the bottle and raised my arms. Flames were all over me. I could smell my hair burning, my cheek being singed. Jay managed to heave himself up and slap at the flames with me. Together we put them out.

I sat down, all strength drained out of me, and I could think only of how lucky I had been to take along that silly cap. Without it my long, curly hair would have gone up in flames.

I told myself that this was a bad dream, a nightmare, and I wanted out of it. *Now. No more. I've had enough. Somebody shake me awake.* But the only way out was to go for more gas, to make the trip again and again and again, for as long as it would take. *You are not hurt,* I said to myself. *You are okay.* And with that I got up and went for another bottle of gas.

We didn't notice the breeze at first. It began ever so gently, causing the fire to sway and dance. Little by little it took over control of the flames so that we never quite knew in what direction they would blow. I told myself to be more alert, even more careful. Now that we had to outwit the wind, my firetending job would require some skill.

In one of my brief respites I sat down on a rock and forgot to pull my skirt under me. Only my nylon slip was between my bare skin and the rock, and it felt wonderfully good. *Imagine that,* I thought. *How nice that rock feels on my naked rear. Why does it feel so good, Lauren?* The answer came like a light bulb in a comic strip: *It feels good because it is warm.*

74

"Jay," I yelped, "the rocks. They hold the heat. We can put them in our pockets and keep our hands warm, and we can stack them by our feet. We can build up a whole pile of them and set them on fire and they'll give off heat like a regular radiator."

I was overjoyed at my discovery. I quickly began gathering medium-sized rocks to stack up, smashing my fingers a couple of times. If we sprayed the rocks enough, burned a lot of gas all over them, they should get very hot and offer another source of heat—a kind of second line of defense.

"Help me," I called to Jay. "The more we can heat up, the better off we'll be. Don't you see how important it is?"

Jay lifted himself on an arm, the way he did when he had to throw gas on the fire. For a minute I saw him make what seemed to be an effort, but then he sank back against the door. He had moved very little since the fire had started, and that was five or six hours ago.

My anger spilled over. "Look," I spat out at him, "the least you can do is keep your hands in your pockets or under your armpits. You're all spread out, which means you're losing body heat. The least you can do is take care of yourself, damn it."

I was nagging and I hated it; Jay hated it too. Every time I told him to do something he would grunt. The sound would say, as clearly as anything, "Leave me alone." I wondered why I couldn't just let him be. Why did I feel so compelled to remind him, over and over again, to take care of himself?

I managed, finally, to get about two dozen rocks into a pile. The wind was rising in earnest now, and it was all we could do to keep the gas trained on the pile of rocks. There was no longer a steady flame; the wind put the fire through crazy paces, tossing whirlwinds of flame into the air and blowing them out.

I hoped it was two o'clock, at least. That would mean six hours of darkness had already passed, with four or five more to go. The thought was too much. I could not fathom another five hours so I backed away from it. *Think of the next trip for fuel,* I told myself, *no more. Go step by step, rock by rock.* I made six, seven more trips. It seemed that I had spent my whole life feeding that insatiable fire. The night had no end; I would go on forever, climbing back and forth, fighting the wind.

I handed Jay a beer bottle filled with gas, threw my stream on the fire, and went back under the wing for another bottle. Jay was supposed to build up the flame so that I could see under the wing, but I noticed that it was growing particularly dim.

"Jay, get on top of it," I yelled. Then I waited for a burst of light. When it didn't come I looked back. The fire was dangerously low. I scrambled back with my full bottle, shouting at him all the while. Both of us began to pour gas on the remaining fire. It sizzled and disappeared. We waited for the rallying burst of flame that had come so many times before.

This time it didn't happen. This time the fire was out.

7

It was as if light no longer existed. An implacable blackness flooded the mountaintop, rising like an ocean to obliterate all vision. The dark and cold swallowed us, and for an instant I felt the immensity of the knowledge that we were isolated and that the isolation was inviolate.

The fire was out, the light was gone, and the cold scorched my breathing. *Think,* I told myself. I reached out to touch Jay, to make sure he was there, next to me. He was there.

I thought: *Okay, back to the cigarette lighter.* It had to work one more time. I got up. My skirt was again stuck to the skin on my thigh, and I carefully peeled the soft wool away, wincing as it came unstuck from my skin. Then I smoothed my skirt before crawling over Jay to get to the forward seat of the plane.

"The cigarette lighter," I said as I passed over his body, accidentally poking him in the chest.

"Uh," he groaned.

"Sorry," I answered automatically.

In the cockpit I threw the switch that activated the battery and was immensely relieved to hear the reassuring whir. I pushed in the cigarette lighter and waited. My fingers were still numb and clumsy, and I blew on them to keep them moving. I waited for what seemed the right length of time. When the lighter did not pop out I decided my time sense must be off, so I waited some more. Minutes passed. Finally I felt for the instrument panel and traced it with my fingers until I found the lighter. I jerked it out, but no color glowed in the darkness, no orange, nothing. I put my finger on the part that should have been glowing. It was not even warm.

The lighter had *to work, that was all there was to it,* I thought. I punched it in again as firmly as I could. The darkness was total in the cockpit, and I fumbled as I pushed the lighter in and pulled it out. I punched it in a dozen times before I yelled to Jay.

"You try," I said, figuring that I had to be doing something wrong, that I must have forgotten some very simple little thing that would make the lighter work. It might work again for Jay. "You have to try," I yelled, thinking that if I were firm enough I could jar him out of his lethargy.

I suppose I knew he wouldn't try; I knew it even before he turned me down in the same flat tone that had not varied in hours. Jay had stationed himself on the one comfortable spot when the fire started and he had hardly moved since, except for the times when I set us ablaze. He had rallied then, but he didn't seem to want to be bothered now. Either that or he knew it was no use—the way he had known the radio wasn't working—and hadn't the heart to tell me. Perhaps he had even known about Jean, that there was no hope for her.

Anyway, the fire was out and I couldn't get it started again. Probably Jay couldn't get it going either, I reasoned. Even if he did manage to do it the wind was coming up in earnest, and we would have a terrible time trying to control a fire in that kind of wind.

So much for Plan A, I said to myself. *What is Plan B?* Clearly, I would have to settle for an alternative course of action. Then I remembered the second line of defense—the rocks. What we had was a pile of very hot granite rocks that would give off heat for a time, maybe for a long time. The heat would last longer if I could get the rocks into a small, protected space out of the wind. I decided to load them into the tail section of the plane, the part that had partially split off from the main body. It was a small aluminum cone just big enough for two bodies and a store of heated granite.

"If we get in there," I said to Jay, "I mean, if we pile some rocks into the tail of the plane—" I knew I had asked him the question several times before, but clearly the idea bothered me. "If we pile in all those rocks and ourselves in after," I started over again, "do you suppose we might tip it over?" I could imagine the plane tumbling down the mountain.

"It's okay," he said with unconcealed annoyance. "It's anchored. The wingtip is dug in. The wheels too." He answered as if by rote. There was a tape-recorded quality to his voice, and it gave me the bizarre feeling that in some way he wasn't there.

The thought crossed my mind: *Is he leaving?* Leaving, slipping away. Could something be wrong with him that I didn't understand?

No, I told myself firmly. I had survived the crash and so had Jay. All I had to think about was keeping warm. Jay said the plane was solidly anchored. I sincerely hoped he was right.

I squeezed sideways through the tiny baggage door and kicked out some flimsy plastic dividers used to separate the compartment. Our feet would be near the bottom, where the fuselage narrowed at the tail of the plane, and our heads would be at the top. The roof had split open, exposing the rear passenger seat; but if we curled as low as we could, we would be well enough protected.

"We've got to pile as many rocks into the tail as we can," I ordered as I climbed back out. "There's enough room for the two of us, and we've got to fill the leftover space with stones. Maybe they'll get us through what's left of the night."

Jay said nothing, and he did not move. I resisted the urge to say something cutting. It would take too much energy and I had to gather the stones.

I began to grope in the dark, feeling for the hot, oil-blackened stones. I smelled flesh singeing, felt the stinging pain in my hands. I bit my lip and held on to the burning rocks. *The hotter the better,* I thought. My left arm was of little use, but I managed to get several rocks into the tail. A fingernail bent back and broke off, and my fingers were smashed and charred; but it was the price I had to pay, I told myself. The rocks were all the insurance we had.

Each time I hefted a piece of granite through the baggage door I noticed the tail section shift perceptibly. I wondered how many pounds it would take to dislodge the plane and send it in an avalanche, with bits of plane and bits of bodies strewn down the mountainside.

Stop it! I lashed out at myself. *Don't waste energy on those things that are beyond you.* Then I curled into the bottom of the cone with the rocks I had gathered: one at my head, several at my feet, one for my bottom and another for my back, and one tucked warm into my stomach, my arms and hands wrapped around it.

For the first time in what seemed an eternity I felt almost comfortable. The rocks had warmed my aluminum nest remarkably well. The wind whistled outside, but it seemed removed. I was snuggled in like a squirrel, and it wasn't bad at all.

"Jay," I called out, "it really is warm and nice in here. Crawl in with me." I knew it would be a snug fit—like two bodies curled into a big laundry basket—but his additional body heat could only make it better.

Jay didn't answer. I figured he was hunkered down over the pile of hot rocks that remained outside. They were probably giving off plenty of heat, but the wind was blowing and they wouldn't stay warm for long.

I let myself float, basking in the unexpected comfort. It felt wonderful not to have to tend the fire, not to have to make the interminable trips back and forth to gather gasoline. But little by little a thought began to nag at me, the kind that comes on a cold winter's night when you know you are going to need another blanket but you hate the idea of getting out of a warm bed to get it. Soon, I knew, I had to crawl back out and put as many more rocks as I could into this aluminum cocoon, because I had no idea how many would be *enough*. I didn't know if all the heated rocks on this frigid mountain would be *enough*. I didn't know if all the heated rocks in the blessed world would be *enough*. I just knew I had to gather more—and quickly, before they lost their heat.

I heard Jay just outside the baggage door. He was up and moving! *Glory hallelujah,* I thought. *He's finally decided to do something.* He could hand me some stones and I wouldn't have to go out in the cold again after all.

I yelled out to him, "As long as you're there, hand me a few more rocks, would you?"

The wind wailed and Jay was moving, but he didn't answer. I twisted until I could make out the vague outline of his form through the baggage door.

"Please, Jay, just hand them to me here, through the door. You're right there, you could."

"No," he said, adding something else I couldn't hear, but I got the message.

"Damn it, Jay, it won't hurt you to hand me a few more

rocks. Come on." When I heard myself beginning to whine, I stopped. *To hell,* I thought, *just to hell.*

I heard Jay lumber into the front of the plane, felt the fuselage teeter as he dragged himself in. The wind had begun to whistle into the loose crevices, and some pieces of metal were banging against the plane. I was going to have to get out, and the thought was agonizing. As I pulled myself to a sitting position, I could see Jay sprawled across the front seat of the plane. He was hugging a warm rock to his stomach. *Well,* I thought, disgusted, *at least he managed to do something for himself.*

I sighed and squeezed out the door like a miserable cat banished into the cold and began my search for more rocks. It was even harder this time; there seemed to be fewer of them and they were heavy. My left arm was giving me trouble. I groped around in the dark, feeling the stones to see if I could lift them to my hip and then work my way back to the plane with them.

Suddenly I had to pee. The idea struck me as peculiar. When I thought about it, I realized that quite a few of my normal body functions seemed to have shut down. I had not felt hungry and I hadn't needed to eliminate. I hadn't even felt particularly thirsty. Then I remembered the quantities of beer we had downed, and I was a little surprised that I hadn't needed to go sooner.

My hand explored a nice warm rock that was too big to move. I lifted my skirt, careful to pull the fabric of both slip and skirt away from me so it wouldn't get wet and freeze. I sat on the rock, enjoying its heat, and spread my legs. What had been warmly held inside my body was now out on the cold granite and would be ice within minutes. The thought made me push on to struggle with rocks hotter and larger than I might have tackled a few moments before. *The margin will be small,* I cautioned myself. *There is no room for error.*

I am not sure how long it took me to gather six more rocks

and return to my aluminum nest. It seemed forever, but it was worth it because the added heat was immediately noticeable. The air in the section was almost warm, and I was content that I had done all I could do. With that thought I pulled my silk scarf over my face and curled into a fetal position. *Lauren,* I congratulated myself, *you really are smart.*

That is how I felt—smart. I don't mean intelligent or bright or any of the usual meanings of the word. I mean, simply, that given a certain set of conditions I had chosen the proper sequence, I had made optimum use of the possibilities presented. I had put the puzzle together in the time allotted. True, I had come close to blowing it when I made the premature attempt down the mountain. But I had managed, with a large chunk of luck, to correct that error in time.

One thing disturbed me, and that was Jay. I had come to feel responsible for him and I resented it. I couldn't understand: He had come through the crash able to get around, yet he resisted doing anything to help us. I wished I could dismiss him and let him take care of himself, but I couldn't. I really don't know why, but I felt I had to help him. Maybe it was simply that I was so certain my survival was linked to his. We had made a promise, a pact, to get through this night together, to help each other. The pact had been my idea, true; I had pushed him into it, sure that once he had promised I could hold him to it. Maybe it was just that I believe in keeping promises.

Anyway, I called out to Jay once again to lie down next to me. Some time later I felt the plane shudder and knew he was moving. Slowly, laboriously, he dragged himself between the front seats and over the rear one so he could lower himself into my cone-shaped burrow in the tail of the plane.

I thought back to the morning when I had watched him hoist himself easily into the pilot's seat, and I remembered that he had looked like a man swinging onto a horse. His long body had been so graceful, but that agility had disappeared. He slumped down from above, stiff, almost brittle, as if he couldn't bend or sway, as if he were made of metal with hinges for joints. He jammed his rigid body into my nest, ramming his feet into my lap, oblivious to me. The first thing I noticed was that one of his shoes was missing.

"Your shoe!" I blurted, shocked. "What happened to your shoe?"

"It's okay," he mumbled, as if to say it was a small matter that he had lost a shoe. I couldn't believe he didn't realize how important it was to keep every bit of protection, that even a tennis shoe could make a critical difference. It was the extremities—hands and feet—that stood the greatest chance of becoming frostbitten. He could lose some toes, maybe even his foot! My God, how could I make him understand how serious it was?

"Forget it," he muttered irritably. He was thrashing around, trying to get comfortable, knocking his elbow into my cheek and my head, pummeling me with his knees. The plane rocked as he thrashed about. I had visualized us curled up together, our bodies curved to share the heat of the rocks and of each other, cradled together like spoons. I should have known better. Jay tossed and turned, pushing me to get himself into a position in which he was extended rather than curled up. I could do nothing except wish with a passion that I had not asked him to join me, that I had left him in the front of the plane by himself.

I grunted and Jay moaned. Our arms and legs were hopelessly tangled. I could feel the plane tilt and shift with his clumsy movements. I was terrified. "You've got to stop this," I yelped. "Stop it right now! You're going to kill us!"

For a time he was quiet, but then he began to squirm again. Finally we were in a position that was not entirely satisfactory to either of us, but it would have to work. Our legs were intertwined—mine drawn up as much as they could be and his stretched out. When I curled into my squirrel-tuck position, my head came to rest just above his belt buckle. I realized that while my head was well protected, Jay's head and shoulders were exposed in the open section. I could do nothing about it and I didn't try; I didn't want to start Jay moving again.

Instead I nagged. "Do you have your hood pulled up over your head?" I would say. "Keep your face covered; pull your shirt up over it and breathe down onto your chest. I read that fifty percent of body heat is lost through the head." I couldn't remember where I had read it and I had no idea if there was any truth to it. But it was something to say, some way to make contact with Jay, to make him do as much as he could to take care of himself.

For a while I searched my memory for every bit of information I might have stored on how to conserve body heat. In the morning it might be something else, but during the night cold was our enemy.

I chattered on. "Keep your hands tucked somewhere warm. Put them under your armpits or in your belt, somewhere where it's—"

I felt Jay groping under my jacket, reaching down, pushing his hands under the waistband of my skirt and grabbing at my bare flesh. I was furious.

"No!" I hissed. "No!" A chill ran up my spine. "Keep your hands between your own legs, or in your pockets or someplace," I snapped. He withdrew his hands.

I was being practical too. I didn't want him to touch me because his hands were so cold. I had thought he would add heat. Now I was worried that he might withdraw it and I didn't intend to let that happen.

I began to rub his legs and blow on his hands, figuring that if I could get his circulation going better he would warm up. He didn't resist so it must have felt okay. He was quiet for a time after I stopped. I used the interlude to concentrate, asking myself questions which I would then answer, formally, carrying on a kind of simplistic dialogue with myself. *One, two, one, two, wiggle your toes,* I would say. *Don't forget to keep them moving.* Then I would obediently wiggle my toes and think about nothing. But most of the time I concentrated on the need to keep myself centered, balanced. I had to figure out our priorities.

"We must not allow ourselves to go to sleep," I said out loud. "We've got to keep talking, nudging each other every couple of minutes to keep from dozing off. Understand?"

"Yeah," Jay answered with the sourness I had come to expect, but I could tell by his tone that he agreed. I tilted my head back in an effort to see him, but I couldn't make out his face in the dark. I could see the stars above him. They seemed close.

The sky was clear. That meant the day would be sunny—whenever the day came. "They must know about us by now," I blurted out. "They have to know that we are down. They would have figured that out by now. Of course the planes can't take off in the dark, but I figure they'll come for us at daybreak. They'll be here in the morning, first thing. The sun will be out and we can leave the plane and even take a little nap in the sun. It will be warm enough then. We won't have to worry about going to sleep and freezing. They're going to come for us in the morning, I'm sure of it."

I thought about how it would be. A helicopter would land in the basin below us and the men—there would be five or six—would climb up carrying blankets and a thermos full of hot coffee. Steaming hot coffee. The blankets would be red-and-blue plaid with a red fringe, and the hot coffee would feel warm in our bellies. I sighed at the thought of it.

"All we have to do is make it through this night," I told Jay. "I'm sure everything is being put in motion right now. It's just a matter of waiting for the light. Jimmie's got it organized—Jimmie is a great organizer. At dawn they'll come looking for us."

"How long?" Jay wanted to know. "How long before it gets light?"

I looked at the sky. It was still black. Sundown had been about 7:30 and we had kept the fire going for five or six hours. The trouble was that on the mountain there was no way to gauge time. When I worked all night in the studio it was different: As the night progressed I could hear the street grow quiet. And then the cats would begin to get more active as the night began to turn to day. I would hear the first train rumble by on the elevated tracks and the traffic pick up on the freeway behind the studio. But here I knew only that the earth was rotating, that by painful degrees daybreak had to come.

I did not know how long we had been in the plane. Two hours maybe. Possibly three. I hoped it was three o'clock. I knew the next three hours would be critical. The rocks had begun to cool. It would be close.

I didn't answer Jay's question. It didn't seem worth it. Instead, I thought about Jim. I wondered what he was doing at that precise moment.

8

Oakland, California

At 3:20 on the morning of April 27, the phone rang in Jay Fuller's house in El Sobrante, California. Jim Fizdale was sleeping fitfully on Jay's bed, but he picked up the phone before the second ring.

"This is Major Warren at Air Force Rescue Coordination Center," a voice on the other end of the line said. "I want to inform you that we are taking over the search effort for the missing Cessna 182 with a member of your family aboard. I have a few questions."

Jim sat up, swung his legs over the side of the bed, turned on the light, and reached for the sheet of paper that was by now crosshatched with names and numbers and notes.

He had refined the story to a point of precision. After so many tellings he would give Major Warren only those details he knew to be pertinent. He included nothing extraneous. He did not, for example, bother to correct the major's assumption that he was related to Lauren. Instead, he reeled off names and numbers, probable destination, time of departure and estimated time of arrival, probable routes, and those airfields in the area that had been checked. They talked for a time, in questions and answers mostly, keeping it terse and to the point.

At the end of the conversation Jim asked for the major's name and phone number so that he could record them with all the others he had collected through the night. When the man gave an 800 area code, Jim asked, "Where are you anyway?"

"Illinois," the major answered with military briskness. "Air rescue is coordinated from a central location here."

Jim hung up and sank back on Jay's bed, his body aching with exhaustion and tension. From the taste in his mouth he knew he must have been sleeping, at least for a while, though he couldn't remember dozing off. A heavy, dull feeling had settled in his chest. It had been there ever since he had become certain that Lauren and Jay and Jean had crashed.

Now, he thought, *Lauren's fate has been turned over to a central location in Illinois.* Tears squeezed into his eyes. He could feel them sliding down his face and he turned to blot them on Jay's pillow.

After a time he got up and walked to the door of Carla's room. He could hear her breathing, the soft, regular sounds a child makes in deep sleep. Gael moved behind him so quietly that he didn't hear her until she spoke.

"Anything new?" she asked.

Gael Thompson was a good friend. He had known her for years, had introduced her to Lauren, and the two women had become friends too.

"No," he answered. "The call was from some major in Illinois telling me they are taking over the search."

"Isn't that strange?" she asked.

"Yeah," he said. "Things get more and more complicated. I just hope the rescue system is as efficient as they make it sound."

"You look exhausted," Gael told him. "Can you sleep?" Sensing the answer to be no, she quickly added, "I'll make some tea."

At three o'clock on the afternoon of the preceding day, Jim Fizdale had noted the time and thought: *They're probably in the air now, on the way home.* It was a random thought. He didn't think of Lauren again until six o'clock, when he had expected her to be back. He knew they had had a late start and would probably be late in returning. He also knew Jay to be chronically late. But it would be light until about 7:30, so there was plenty of time.

Jim turned on the basketball game—the Phoenix Suns were playing Oakland's Golden State Warriors—and quickly became absorbed in the action. He followed sports with a passion. It was a preoccupation he did not share with Lauren, not that it mattered. Their relationship did not require them to share all interests; it was not based on total togetherness.

The phone rang shortly after seven. It was Carla Fuller, Jay's ten-year-old daughter. "Jimmie," the child said, "Dad isn't home yet. Did Lauren go flying with him today? Do you know where he is?"

He looked at the clock and was annoyed with himself for having lost track of the time. "Lauren did go with them," he answered, "and they're a little late. They probably just got delayed."

"I'm kind of worried," she said. "Dad's late sometimes, but not this—"

"Listen, Carla," he broke in, taking over, "I'm going to check into it. You sit tight and I'll call you right back, okay?"

90

Carla Fuller was a composed child, independent and self-reliant. She shared an easy familiarity with Jim Fizdale. He had spent Christmases and Thanksgivings and gone on outings with the girl and her father, and she trusted him.

Jim looked up the Cal Flying Club in the telephone directory. It had a university prefix, so he assumed there would be no answer if he called. The switchboard closed at five o'clock, he knew, and it was well after that hour now. Instead he called Oakland Airport and was transferred to the Federal Aviation Administration office.

"Kaminski," a man answered.

Jim cleared his throat and with a certain hesitation began to spell out his worry. He tried not to appear overly alarmed. They were, after all, little more than an hour overdue.

"A tall, redheaded guy with a beard?" Kaminski asked. "I remember—he came in this morning. He didn't file a flight plan."

"Is that unusual?" Fizdale asked.

"No," Kaminski answered. "We recommend it but it isn't required. But look, the first thing you've got to know is the kind of craft he's flying and its number. That's essential information, something you need before anybody can begin to look for them."

Jim said he hadn't called the University of California Flying Club, that he didn't think anyone would be there at this hour.

"I'll tell you what," Kaminski offered. "The Cal Flying Club hangar is close to the office here. I'll go over and see what I can find out. I'll call you back in five or ten minutes."

Jim waited, listening for Lauren's key in the lock, convinced that she would walk in the door any minute and everything would be settled. He thought that he would probably feel a little foolish, that maybe he had raised the alarm a bit early. Still, Carla was alone and she was worried. When Lauren got home he would call Carla to let her know Jay was on his way. It wasn't so much that Lauren should have called in, Jim reasoned. It was that Carla was just a kid, after all, and Jay shouldn't have let her worry. He hoped they had a good reason—a very good reason—for not having called. He knew that if they didn't, he was going to be slightly pissed.

The phone jolted him; he half expected it would be Lauren. It was Kaminski.

"One space *is* empty," he reported. "There was a phone number on the door you can call. When you get the number of the plane a ground search can begin—that is, any field where they might have put down will be checked."

Jim didn't say so but he felt sure it wasn't likely. If they had landed in some little airport out in the boondocks there would have been a telephone, and if there had been a telephone Lauren would have called. She would not have kept him hanging; she wasn't like that. Jay wouldn't have left Carla alone this long either.

Carla answered almost before the phone had a chance to ring. "Listen," Jim began, trying to sound reassuring, "I know there's a good reason for their delay but I'm going to come out and stay with you until your dad gets home. If he isn't there by the time I get to your house, I'll make some phone calls and try to find out what's going on. I'll be there in about twenty minutes."

"Okay, Jimmie," the child said, and he could tell she was relieved.

He hung up but sat with his hand on the phone, thinking. Then he dialed Gael's number. "Can you go to Jay's house with me right now?" he asked after briefing her. "Carla's alone, and frankly I'm beginning to feel a little scared, like something could be terribly wrong."

Gael hesitated. She told him she had made other plans. Then she asked, "Is it important?"

"Yes it is," he replied.

"Then I can be ready in five minutes," she said.

He was sure she would be.

They arrived at Jay's house shortly before nine. There Jim began to make a serious effort to discover what had happened to prevent Jay Fuller, Jean Noller, and Lauren Elder from returning to Oakland on schedule. He went through Jay's desk—it was as cluttered as his desk at the vet hospital—and found numbers for some people in the Cal Flying Club. After three or four calls he reached a woman who told him that Jay had checked out a Cessna 182, number N52855. She said they had taken off at about 12:00.

They were now more than two hours overdue, and there had been no word. Jim called the FAA at Oakland Flight Services and was given the names and numbers of the airports in the Death Valley region, in case Jay might have landed at one of them. He added the telephone numbers to those he had already collected, scrawling them on the back of a dance poster: the flight service in Tonopah, Nevada; Furnace Creek Inn; Stovepipe Wells; the National Park Service.

The park service people had been extremely helpful. Until he talked to them, Jim had not fully realized that Jay had chosen to fly over some of the roughest country in America. If Jay had crossed at Kearsarge Pass, as they assumed, he had flown over a section of the High Sierra so rugged that no roads cross the north-south divide for 200 miles. A ranger had explained that much of their route would have crossed national park territory, which meant that there were no ranches and few roads, and that very few people would be in that wilderness at this time of year.

Gael went through the refrigerator and cupboards and put together some supper for Jim and Carla. The child looked tired and worried and she picked at her food. Jim had moved the phone to the floor to avoid disturbing Jay's papers. He ate distractedly, between phone calls. The telephone was ringing with a kind of regularity now, Jim alternating between calling out and waiting for calls to come in.

The child sat on the couch, following the events until Jim told her it was time to go to bed. She went without objection. Gael was with her and Jim could hear them talking, Gael reassuring Carla that there was probably a very good reason for the delay, that everything would be okay by tomorrow.

After Carla was settled, Gael joined Jim in the living room. It was a small house, with knotty pine walls and low ceilings. Jay had furnished it comfortably, and it occurred to Jim that the house was as much without pretension as Jay himself.

As the night wore on, he told the story over and over, adding the small bits of information that came in. Jim now knew that the last radio contact had been with Fresno tower early in the afternoon; Jay had reported he was heading east at 9,000 feet and had asked for a weather report. Jim repeated things like that.

At about two in the morning the calls dwindled. Jim had been in touch with everyone who might aid the search, with the exception of Lauren's parents. He decided to wait until morning to contact them. Maybe it would all be over by then and he wouldn't have to put them through the agony of waiting, of not knowing.

At 2:10 Gael suggested he go into Jay's room to try to get some sleep. She said that he might still have a long ordeal ahead, that he would need some rest. At 2:24 the FAA issued an alert for the aircraft; at 3:20 Major Warren called from Illinois to say the Air Rescue Center would be taking over the search effort; at 3:48 they established a search mission number for the aircraft, now presumed down somewhere between Fresno, California, and the Death Valley National Monument.

Sitting with Gael, sipping tea, Jim tried to reconstruct his conversations of the night and early morning.

"I didn't really understand all the jargon," he told her. "Something about a plane—a C-130, I think—with equipment that can hone in on the ELT." He paused, trying to get it precisely right. "The electronic location transmitter—it's a device that is standard safety equipment on planes. It's in the tail section and it has its own power source. Sometimes it activates on impact, or it can be manually activated. Anyway, it will continue to give off a signal to guide searchers to the crash site. The C-130 follows the expected flight route and tries to pick up the ELT signal."

"When do they start?" Gael asked.

"When it gets light enough to fly," Jim answered. "Then planes will be going out from McClellan Air Force Base— from other places too. I don't know exactly how many people take part in a search like this, but I somehow got the idea that there would be about a dozen planes up there looking for them."

They talked details, hard and practical, because it was easier to deal with facts than with fears, and Jim Fizdale's fears were threatening to overtake him. One question, particularly, had begun to form in his mind. He tried to push it back, tried not to have to confront it.

Gael sensed something specific was on his mind. "What is it?" she probed.

"He said they would search along the *expected* flight route," Jim blurted. "Well, what if Jay didn't cross the Sierras at Kearsarge Pass? What if he went south of there or north? What if he missed the pass somehow?" He was edging closer to the question, the real source of his fear. He lowered his head and said, "They're out there somewhere. They've crashed, that's all but sure. They're out there God knows where. What if they can't find them in time?"

The Second Day

9

"Fire and fleet and candlelights, And Criste receive thy saule." "My candle burns at both ends, It will not last the night." "It's always darkest before the dawn." "Grin and bear it."

Bits and pieces—phrases from ballads and poems and clichés—popped in and out of my mind. Fragments piled one on the other with what seemed no reason, floating up from nowhere.

It was getting colder. The rocks were not entirely cold yet, not enough to pull heat from our bodies, but neither were they warm. The temperature was falling steadily, but it was only a matter of time before the sun came out to run the cold away.

"Come on, sun," Jay whined. "God, I'm so cold." He said it over and over again, unable to contain his impatience. I could not convince him that complaining was a waste of energy; nothing I could say seemed to have any effect. "Where the hell is the sun?" he would wail.

Sometimes I would try to placate him, saying things like, "It's okay, Jay, it won't be too much longer," trying not to sound patronizing. But mostly I would tell him to keep his hands tucked in. "Stamp your feet," I would order. "Move your toes, cover your face." Even to myself I sounded like an obsessive drill sergeant.

"Yeah, yeah," he would grunt, as if I were scolding him, as if I were some shrill old crone whose sole purpose in life was to make him miserable. Then he would whine, "When is this night going to end?"

It was not so much what Jay had done that infuriated me; it was what he hadn't done. He had made a hard situation a lot harder for me by refusing to move. I was not in a mood to be charitable to him. I doubted that I would have much contact with him after this was all over. Still, I wondered how I would feel about him. We had shared a curious sort of intimacy: We had lived through a plane crash together, an experience not many people have. We had been nothing to each other before the crash. It seemed odd that we would return to being nothing to each other when we finally got back to Oakland—odd because of the intensity of what we were going through, what we had already been through.

After a while Jay said, "It's getting lighter, I swear it."

He sounded so convinced that I poked my face out of the scarf to have a look. Bending back slightly, I could see that the black had become a very dark gray. Jay was right; the stars glittered cold in the sky and the wind howled, but the sky was getting lighter.

I imagined what it would be like when the sun came out and heated the thin metal of the plane. We would be warm again. Oh, God, to be warm again! The bitter, black cold would be banished and we would be okay. A line stuck in my head and played over and over, like all the other fragments: *We will be okay if we make it to the day.*

"The hard part is over," I said into my scarf. "It's got to be." Then I closed back into my knot again, pulling in arms and legs, wondering why I didn't ache from having been in that cramped position so long. The cold permeated; it seeped into the pores; it was all there was and all I could think about.

I made myself as small as possible. Jay was more exposed to the wind than I was, and I figured that was why the cold seemed so much more agonizing to him. Suddenly I began to shiver. I could not control my mouth or my teeth, and strange ˌwhoofing noises began to puff out of me as my body started to tremble.

"Is shivering bad for you?" I managed to chatter the words out. "Should I try to stop it?"

" 'S okay," Jay answered. "You're supposed to shiver."

I determined to concentrate on something else besides the cold, something simple. *Breathe in and breathe out,* I told myself. *Watch your breathing.* I superimposed a count to keep my toes moving, my feet stamping. *One and two and in and out.* It worked.

After a time I risked another look at the sky. It *was* getting lighter, though I was exasperated by the number of shades of gray it had gone through already.

"We're getting there," I called out to Jay. "We're going to make it."

He didn't answer. Not a grunt, nothing.

"Jay," I called to him in the tone that meant "Damn it, answer me!"

"Uhhh," he said.

"We're going to make it, aren't we?" It had become a ritual question, part of the litany we had invented during the night. He did not even have to think of the response.

101

"Yeah, we're going to," he said, correctly.

Blessed are they that mourn: for they shall be comforted. Blessed are the meek: for they shall inherit the earth. Blessed are the pure in heart . . . Ave Maria, full of grace.

The thought crossed my mind: *What if he refuses to answer altogether? What if he digs in his heels and won't talk to me anymore? What will I do then?*

The thought slipped away. If the minutes had dragged during the night, they seemed now to have come to a standstill.

I tried again to drag my mind away from the cold, away from the time. I tried to sort out sounds. I had heard three jets in the early morning hours, but now all I could hear was the wind, loud and wailing.

Light is peculiar on a mountaintop. It has strange tones, at the same time more intense and more subtle than those at lower altitudes. At dawn the shades of gray should move to full light. Yet when I looked up there was a curious paleness above me—no stars, only an opaque, milky lightness. Only the wind blowing fiercely in this pearl-white glow.

I pulled myself to a sitting position so I could see out. There was no sun, no sky, no mountain, no valley, no airplane—nothing but fine, icy particles whirling in a crazy thickness, white and blowing in every direction. We were in the midst of a monstrous snowstorm, a blizzard that blotted out everything.

I sank back into my small, cold space, shocked and confused, thoughts whirling inside my head like the snowstorm without. All night long we had watched the stars; it had been clear. Now this. It was surreal, a swirling vortex of whiteness that threatened to pull us in and under.

We had survived the night passage only to be snowed in at dawn. The stones were cool to the touch now, their heat dissipated. Soon they would be as they had been before we came—cold, hard and cold.

A kind of panic had overtaken Jay. His complaining had

diminished, though he still grunted and moaned and kicked me now and then. When he became aware that it was strangely bright, he threw his head back into the open, into the swirling snow. I could hear him howl—with rage, with pain, with fear. Then he began to move, to make heavy, thrashing motions. I drew myself into as small a space as I could to give him room to turn over. He managed to get on his stomach, but it was not what he wanted. He floundered helplessly, as if he had lost all coordination.

"I've got to get out of here," he gasped. "I've got to *do* something."

"There's nothing to do," I shouted back at him, trying to make myself heard over the roar of the storm. "The snow and the wind," I shouted. "You can't get a fire going; we have no matches. There's nothing to do but stay where we are."

"*Got* to do something," he insisted, his voice becoming petulant, demanding. "You do something—*you* help me. You've got to."

"Help yourself," I snapped. If he wanted to go out in the snowstorm, let him.

"I've got to get out of here," he pleaded. "Help me."

Finally I said, "Look, it's stupid to go out there, but if you're going you have to do it by yourself. It's not that hard." He had poked and jabbed and pounded me all night long. I was cold and shaken and it was snowing and I didn't know what was going on. I didn't really care if he crawled out of the plane. I simply wanted him to be still.

"It's easy enough," I repeated. "Grab the seat and pull yourself up with your hands. I'll line up your feet with the ribbing of the fuselage so you can push."

As carefully as I could, I put his feet into position. My hands were so cold that it was hard to feel anything. Even so, Jay's foot—clad only in a thin nylon sock—felt chilly to my touch. There was no warmth left in the plane. The only warmth was in our bodies, and the sun was on the other side of the snowstorm.

"Okay, you're ready. Push!" I yelled. "Pull with your arms and push with your feet." It should not have been hard, but Jay couldn't seem to manage.

"Pull and push." I tried again, thinking that maybe he hadn't got the idea.

"I can't," he called back to me. He was quiet for a long minute, and then he said, "I can't feel anything." There was a frantic edge to his voice.

"I know," I told him, as patiently as I could. "I'm cold too. The cold makes you numb. Look, Jay, it's crazy to go outside anyway. Everything is ice and snow out there. It isn't going to be any better; it'll be worse. All we can do is stay where we are and wait. So shut up and keep still."

Wait, I thought. *Wait for what?* I didn't know. The question was too large to deal with.

"I can't wait," Jay said, whining again. "We've got to do something."

"No," I answered, determined not to waste any more breath on him. "Lie still and shut up."

He erupted in a new spurt of action, more frenzied than before. He began twisting and turning, kicking and punching, all the while crying loudly that we had to do something.

"You've got to," he kept saying. Then he began to beat his hands against the sides of the plane. I could hear them hit the metal, strong, blunt blows that sounded hard. He cried out, his legs hitting me stiffly, his arms banging hard above me, rocking us back and forth even as the wind whistled and the snow whirled.

I had to stop him. His body was turned away from me, and I stared at his back. I knotted my hands into fists and began to pound on his back and his rear. I hit him as hard as I could. I hit him again and again, bringing both fists down on him, meaning to hurt.

104

"Aaagh," he moaned in a thick voice, "you're hurting me." His tone was petulant, childish.

Damn you, I thought, *damn you for making me do this to you, making me hurt you.* Couldn't he see that he was only making things worse? He was making things as bad as they could be. "Couldn't you just be quiet? Couldn't you just shut up and lie still?" I heard a fierceness in my voice that I knew was desperation.

Still he struggled. There was nothing I could do to stop it, nothing but withdraw, physically and emotionally. *Good night and amen. Peace be with you.* I squeezed as far to the bottom of the cone as I could and pulled away from the man flailing in anger and frustration. He was only inches from me, but he might as well have been on another planet. *It cannot get worse,* I thought. *It can only get better.*

In a matter of minutes, as if my prophecy had come true, Jay stopped struggling. He was quiet and I was grateful for it. All I could hear were the echoes of the wind. I did not move for fear of jostling Jay and sending him into another paroxysm of movement. When I thought it was safe I pulled the scarf from my face and looked up. It was snowing still, but now and then I could see little patches of blue between the swirls, and it seemed to be getting brighter.

In his frantic struggles Jay had pulled his pants legs up, exposing his calves. Now that I could see, I reached out to pull down his levis. My wrist brushed against his leg. *Isn't he cold?* I thought.

An uneasy feeling moved into my chest. I pushed the scarf from my face; I could see Jay lying with his head cradled on his arm. It was fully light now. I noticed that his auburn hair was powdered with a fine white snow.

Then I saw his hands. They were bloodied, torn. In his struggles he had beaten them against the metal sides of the plane; they were a mass of scraped flesh. *Dear God,* I thought, *what has he done to himself?*

I pulled myself up to examine his wounds, to see if there was anything to be done about them. I reached out to touch his arm and I heard the sound—a small, sharp, sucking intake of breath, a gasp—before I realized I had made it.

Jay's arm was frozen. The flesh was hard and cold and frozen, solid.

I looked at it for a long time, looked at the watch that bound the frozen wrist, stopped at 2:15 the day before.

Only minutes ago he had been calling out to me to do something. "I can't feel anything," he had said. But I hadn't thought, hadn't known. *Oh, Jay.*

I turned him gently, carefully, and he rolled away from me. The wound on his forehead had been reopened; he must have hit his head against the plane. I stared at the wound. Blood had frozen even as it had seeped out, so that it looked like a mass of carmine-colored worms frozen in midmotion and piled on his brow.

I put my hand to his neck, feeling for the jugular. No surge, no throbbing pulse. I had to be sure. I slipped my hand under his shirt, probing for a heartbeat. There was none.

The wind whined and wrapped itself around the carcass of the plane, ruffling Jay's snow-powdered hair in the first light of day. I sat there for a long time, looking at him. His eyes were open and staring.

I had not thought he would die.

I had not known that was what it was like to die.

10

Jay had kept his promise. He said we would get through the night together, that we would make it to the day. He had stayed with me. I looked at his face, at his staring eyes, and I thought that now he was out of the cold.

So, I said to myself, *that is how it is.* I had never seen anyone die before. I did not know that it was so—easy. Jay had been talking to me and then he was dead.

His death surprised me; it did not frighten me. Instead, I was filled with a kind of wonder. Jay looked as if all the hurt and turmoil were over, all the worry and the not knowing. He looked as if he had managed to end the struggle. It would be so very, very nice to be out of the cold. And it would be so easy.

His body was freezing; he would be totally rigid before long, I knew. I looked up and again noticed a few patches of blue in the blowing snow. I had never experienced a storm like it. The snow seemed not to fall, but to come from every direction at once. It filtered onto Jay's face and beard, dusting it with a fine powder, like sugar.

I could do nothing but wait. I had no choice but to curl up once more, next to Jay's stiff legs.

I thought that maybe I could just doze off for a while. It would be so easy, so easy. I felt drowsy enough. If I went to sleep I wouldn't have to remember to wiggle my toes and stamp my feet. I would be rid of the cold and the pain. All I had to do was close my eyes and let the drowsiness take me, let it lift me up and take me in, let it wrap around me like a blanket, warm and nice.

I knew that people had been snowbound in these mountains before. I knew that sometimes it snowed for days on end. Planes couldn't fly; helicopters couldn't land; no one could see in this kind of driving snow. Everything depended on how long the storm lasted. Nobody could control it; nobody could do anything but wait for it to lift. When the search party came they would find Jean on the rocks below us, dead. And they would find Jay lodged in this aluminum cone, dead. I imagined how they would find me, huddled in a fetal position. They would try to twist into this space and maybe they would reach for a pulse, as I had reached for Jay's. And maybe I would be frozen and grotesque.

The thought disturbed me. It seemed like such a waste, such a careless way to die. *The point,* I told myself as I lay next to Jay's dead and freezing body, *is that I am talking about suicide.* To give up would be the easy way out. And the obstacles were overwhelming. So much depended on forces beyond my control. The line, so thin for so many hours, was barely discernible. I knew that.

Still, I thought, my mother shouldn't have to live with the knowledge that her only daughter had frozen in the fetal position, buried in a broken plane on the top of a high mountain.

My mother's brother had died in a small plane when the wings iced over. I didn't want her to go through that again.

And I had so much left to do. I had hardly even begun. There were so many places I had not been, so many people I had not met, so much work to be done. I had not laughed enough or learned enough or felt enough. I had not borne a child. *No,* I said to myself. *Not yet. Not now.*

I reached as far down in the plane as I could, and I began to work Jay's socks off his feet. It was surprisingly easy. Then I unzipped my boots and took my feet out. The force of the cold was stunning. *Wiggle one and wiggle two.* The childishness of the command was lost in my need to know my toes would respond. They did, they wiggled, they were still okay.

I slipped on Jay's socks and put my feet back into my boots. The thin nylon socks did not seem like much protection. I was surprised that they made a difference, but they did. My feet felt better.

As I zipped up the boots I realized that it was getting lighter. I pulled the scarf away from my face once more and was greeted by the sun. It was shining brightly. The sky was blue and the snow was gone. I could scarcely believe it. Then suddenly I was aware of a sound other than the wind. It seemed to fade in and out, grow stronger then weaker. It was a plane, a small plane, and it was close.

They were coming for me, I was sure of it! It was the search party, coming to rescue me. I scrambled out of the cold tail section, bumping against Jay's body, hurrying. *Oh, Jay, I'm so sorry, so damned sorry you couldn't wait.*

But I had made it; it was morning and the sun was out. I ignored the cold and the stiffness that permeated my body and hoisted myself out of the plane.

The airplane was flying over a mountain ridge to the south, not far from me but not close either. My heart jumped as I thought of the pilot flying the plane—alive and close. *Please,* I thought, *please fly this way.*

I leaped and shouted and waved my arms. And I watched as the plane moved farther and farther away, until it was finally out of sight.

He had not seen me. He would have signaled, would have flown back over the wreckage and dipped his wings. He would have done something to let me know help was on its way.

If he had seen me he would not have flown away.

11

He didn't see me. The pilot of the plane was flying high, high and straight; he wasn't circling. Probably he wasn't even looking for us. Probably he was some rancher on his way to Owens Valley, flying his private plane.

I stood in the early morning light, shivering in the bitter-cold wind. It was like all the miserable bus corners I had stood on in the East, waiting in a winter's wind, waiting until my knees turned purple. Waiting, that was the worst of it. I couldn't stay in the open; I had to get out of the wind.

My thinking wasn't especially incisive. Unlike the night before, I had no plan of action. Once again, I considered the possibilities: I could crawl back into the plane alongside Jay's body, but I didn't want to do that. I needed more clothes. I had taken Jay's socks and I would have taken his jeans and jacket too, if I could have managed to get them off. I would have taken them without hesitation, knowing it was the *cor-*

rect thing to do. He was dead. I had been careful to be sure of it.

I thought about Jean's down jacket, but to get it I would have to go down the mountain looking for her. I would have to confront her body and I couldn't, I just couldn't. Besides, I told myself, the jacket would be frozen and as the sun grew stronger it would thaw and be wet.

I scanned the tree line below me to the west. The trees would protect me from the wind, but it would be a long hike down. And once there I couldn't be seen from the air. Miles and miles of wilderness lay between the mountaintop on which I was stranded and the San Joaquin Valley. I doubted that I would ever find my way out if I headed west.

That left the steep eastern slope, the one I had failed to descend the afternoon before. Remembering, I shuddered. But the granite outcroppings of rock on the crest would shut out the westerly wind, and if I stayed on top I could be seen. So the rocks seemed the best temporary answer.

I climbed to the top, the wind at my back, urging me on. I was breathing hard and my hands were numb with the cold, but my legs were working. I crawled behind a massive chunk of granite perched at the crest. I was out of the wind. The sun was rising, and I was sitting at the top of the world, blowing on my fingers, trying to get them to move again.

My hands were raw and rough. The pores had filled with oily grime from the gasoline, the nails were broken, and the skin was a fishbelly white. I rubbed them against my arms until I could feel my fingers begin to flex.

As the first rays of sunlight soaked into me, I scanned the terrain below, thankful to be out of the wind and out of the plane, thankful to be sitting there, alive, in the morning sun. Below me was a steep, almost vertical drop for what looked to be a few hundred feet. It was impossible to tell from above just how far it went before it tapered off into the bowl. I knew now, from experience, that the angle of descent was deceiving in this snow-and-granite world. The slope was more precipitous than I'd thought.

It was, of course, folly to think of attempting to climb down. I was on the top of what was surely one of the highest mountains in the country. I had dropped from the sky and I was sitting, impaled, on a peak some two miles above sea level. When I looked below me all I could think was that it was the kind of snow cliff that an experienced mountain climber might try to negotiate, equipped with ice picks and boots with cleats and all kinds of paraphernalia.

I studied the first, most hazardous drop calmly, without any thought of attempting another descent. Soon I began to notice that the outcroppings of granite that periodically pushed up through the snow seemed to have a pattern to them. They zigzagged down the northern face of the bowl, like a child's connect-the-dot game. In my mind I began to link the outcroppings together, line by line, to form a crooked path down the mountain. I thought that perhaps I could do it that way, picking my way from rock to rock, moving sideways across and down.

Once I reached the gentler slopes below, it would be easy going, really apple pie. I could see that! The snowfield ended in an expanse of rock that funneled into a single arroyo, a dry, rock-filled stream bed. That would lead straight out to the desert flat. The drainage pattern was wonderfully easy to read. It all but said, "Right this way, folks." I'd been hiking in the country enough to know that the way to get to a safe place is to follow a stream. I'd have no trouble at all, I figured, once I had maneuvered the first horrendous drop.

It occurred to me to try a few experimental steps. The afternoon before, I had tried to head straight down. That had been disastrous. But what if I went down at an angle, diagonally across the face of the cliff? I could move on all fours, doing a kind of sideways spiderwalk, balancing myself on the ice crust, punching through it with my hands and feet. The first outcropping was about a dozen feet away. I knew I could always pull back, could stay put and wait for the search party that was bound to come.

Or was it? In the last hours with Jay I had been so certain that *they* would come for us, bright and early. *They* would land in their helicopter, storm up the hill, and take care of us. In my mind *they* were big, husky lumberjacks, strong and competent. In the full morning light I could admit it was a fantasy. There was a good possibility that *they* would not get to me in time.

Perhaps the alarm had not even been sounded. What if Jim figured we had decided to stay over in Death Valley for the night? What if he had waited until this morning to begin looking for us? Maybe Jay's daughter had gone to someone's house; maybe they decided just to wait and see if Jay turned up today. Maybe, maybe, maybe. That was the hell of waiting on the mountain, not knowing who had done what, or what the likelihood of being found was. The plane that flew over earlier that morning hadn't seen me. The wreckage itself was infinitesimal in the vast panorama of the mountains. And if they couldn't see the plane, how could I expect them to see me?

If the day passed and nobody came, I would have to spend another night on the mountain. I tried to push the thought away but it wouldn't go. Another night in the dark and cold, and this time no fire, no light, no warmth at all. A night huddled next to Jay's dead body. I had to get down, down to the desert where it was warm.

I took a deep breath, pulled the tart air into my lungs, moved my fingers, and carefully, slowly, lowered myself over the edge. I slammed my boot toe through the ice and felt a surge of excitement as it held.

Okay, I said to myself. *One more time.* My right fist smashed through the crust and I winced at the resistance it met, but at the same time I was glad. The ice was thick and

114

hard, much firmer than it had been the day before. It would hold my weight, I was sure of it.

My hands gripped the ice; it was slippery. I would have to be careful. I kept my stomach close in, my butt tucked under, my center of gravity as low as possible. Once more, kick and hold. Smash with a fish and hang on, dear God. Move sideways like a spider, splayed out on the vertical ice-blue slick of the mountain. Careful not to slip, careful not to go careening down into the bowl.

Ever so slowly I crept toward the first rock. It was almost close enough to step on. Another foothold, another handhold, and I had made it. It had taken five moves and my hands were numb, but I had made it. The climb was hard but it was not impossible—and the air was warmer, and the wind was gone.

When I could move my fingers again I started out for the next outcropping. Halfway there, a gust of cold air blew up under my skirt, billowing my wraparound and chilling my bare behind. I yelped but I held on.

The thought popped into my mind: *What if somebody is below, looking up? What if somebody across the way has binoculars and is wondering what this silly woman is doing crawling bare-assed down the face of one of the highest mountains in the West?* I couldn't believe what I was thinking. How crazy! The idea was so ludicrous I wanted to laugh or cry or both. And I might have, had I not thought it would throw me off balance. Instead, I grabbed for the next rock and clung to it, panting. *Modesty!* I snorted. *Incredible.*

At each clump of rock I would cling, panting for breath, holding hard until the pain of exertion began to ebb, until I could breathe again. Then I would rest and chafe my hands, not thinking about my next move, never thinking further than the next rock. I tried not to look out, because then I would see how perilous it was to be clinging to the slick side of this mountaintop. I would see how impossible it was that I should

115

try to go against this terrain. I was one human, infinitesimal in the vast, cold quiet. It made no sense. It was absurd. I would never be able to make it. Yet I *was* making it. Somehow I was.

So I continued moving down from one rock to the next, testing each one first to see if it would break off in my hand (as sometimes happened) and if it was firmly rooted before putting my weight on it. I was careful to stop long enough to warm my fingers and catch my breath, to pull the thin air into my lungs. Then I would move on, punching through the ice, traveling steadily across the snowclad face of the mountain.

Yesterday's fatigue had vanished. I felt rested and filled with a peculiar energy—peculiar because I didn't have the slightest idea where it came from. My broken arm pained only when I twisted it; if I avoided any pivotal motion the hand worked. I favored it some, but not much. The fact was I needed both hands to climb. So, broken bone or not, the arm had to work.

The effort of climbing had warmed my body, except for my hands and feet, which were serving as ice picks. The sun was full out; the sky was a perfect blue. The reflection of sunlight on snow should have produced a blinding glare; instead, the effect was more like a radiance. The sun seemed to saturate the mountain and set it aglow, the way it does at sundown sometimes when even the rocks seem to have a luminescence.

The snow so covered everything that I had no idea how far I had come or if the angle of descent was diminishing. After an hour or so of punching through the ice and clinging, I began to edge out once more—stomach in, as usual—when I realized it didn't feel right. I pulled back and looked harder at the path to the next rock.

Of course! The incline had lessened. It had become gentle enough for me to pull my skirt under me, sit down on the ice, and shove off. I could slip over the hard ice like a human sled. On the first run I almost overshot the mark, but at the last minute I grabbed the rock and jerked myself around, slamming into the side of it before coming to a halt. *Watch it.* I cautioned myself. *Don't get carried away, not now—not yet.*

But it had worked, I knew it. I had managed the hardest part of the journey down. I looked up then and gasped. I had descended an almost vertical ice cliff, had come crawling down the face of that mammoth mountain. I could so easily have been crushed, could so easily have pulled a storm of ice and snow and rock down upon me and been buried and frozen in the avalanche. But it hadn't happened.

Look what you've done, I sang out to myself. I wanted to rush down the mountain, to get home quickly so I could tell everybody, "You'll never believe what happened to me." I was as excited, as high, as I've been in my whole life and it all spilled over.

Exhilarated, I gave a whoop that echoed down the silent pass. Then I scooted off to the next rock, yelling and spinning from rock to rock, glissading over the ice, sometimes turning in circles and having to grab for a rock in the split second before I would have swooped past it.

I could hear the sound of my laughter rippling out and over the snowfield. I was letting go because the hardest part was over, done with. It was all right to feel good now, to have fun. All I had to do was slide down this mountain, down to the desert warmth below. I was going to be okay.

Except it had taken longer than I thought it would, a lot longer. By midmorning I had come only about a third of the way down the snowfield—the hard third, to be sure. But I still had a lot of snow to cover before I got to the arroyo.

Soon I was able to stand up and start sidestepping down the slope. My boots broke through the ice crust and sometimes I would plunge knee-deep into the snow. It would come over my boottops and get packed inside against my feet. It made me uncomfortable, but there was no point stopping to empty the boots; they would quickly fill again. Still, the cold no longer tormented me. I imagined it to be perfect spring skiing weather—sunny and shirtsleeve warm, so long as I kept moving.

I headed straight down the bowl toward the arroyo. I was glad I didn't have to make any decisions about which way to go; clearly, there was only one way out. Soon it was level enough for me to go swinging along, moving my arms in swaths to get the circulation going, striding as broadly as I could in the snow. I was past the point of having to watch every step. If I fell it would no longer be a disaster.

Had a plane flown over just then, the pilot would have sighted one dark moving dot on an expanse of white. The dot would be traveling down the very center of the vast snow-field. If the pilot had circled to come in for a closer look, he would have caught sight of a solitary female swaggering down the mountain as she might have down a boulevard, walking purposefully as if she were late for an appointment.

"Hello!" I would wave as the pilot came closer. "Hello up there!"

And the pilot would say, "Holy Mary, Mother of God! What in the world is a woman in high-heeled boots and a weirdo flying ace cap doing out here, and where the hell does she think she's going?

Then I would smile and laugh and wave at him, wave for all I was worth, and maybe I would even yell out, "I'm going home, fella! That's where I'm going."

Except no plane came. Half the morning was gone and nobody had come looking for me. Maybe Jim was waiting to see if we would turn up. Maybe he hadn't been able to bring himself to report us missing yet. But it didn't really matter anymore. It didn't matter because I was committed now; I was going to get myself out. My lumberjack rescuers evanesced; I was on my own. I quickened my pace a little, thinking about how worried Jim would be. I wished there were a way to let him know I was okay, to ease his mind.

I had managed a kind of rhythmic walk, swaying to keep better balance. My skirt was swinging out as I moved down the mountain. I noticed the glow first on the hemline as it swirled out—a ripple of yellow light, a band that shimmered about the hem of my skirt, swaying with it. It was a brilliant, iridescent light, glowing and sparkling. I watched it, fascinated. Then I noticed an outer band of color, this one magenta, glowing all about my arms. By waving them like wands I could cast beautiful, sparkling ribbons of color in the air. I felt like Tinkerbell.

For a while I played with the color, delighted to be able to create such patterns. But then I began to worry that something might be dreadfully wrong with my eyes. I knew so little about the physiology of the eye, but I had heard of snowblindness and I wondered if it was happening to me, if the reflection of the sun on snow had done some optical damage. Strangely, as soon as I became anxious, the colors vanished.

All along I had been acutely aware of the light in the mountains. Delineations were so much sharper, the colors so much more intense at high elevations. Yet I had been in high mountains before and I had never noticed the color. But then I had not been alone, away from all roads, all people. I had never negotiated a snowfield with a broken arm before either. Nor had I ever survived a plane crash, or seen a person die.

So much was happening to me that I could not be sure what was going on without and what within. Did the rocks truly have an incandescent glow, or was the glow a message relayed from my brain? Or were they one and the same?

I had not yet covered half the snowfield, and I was tired of trudging—tired of the snow in my boots and of being mired down in the snow, tired of keeping my eyes on my feet. I sat on a rock to take a short rest and raised my eyes to scan the mountain. That was when I saw them.

They were curved along a ridge of rocks, directly across from me—a row of houses built of beautifully mellowed redwood, skillfully integrated into the landscape. They looked like chalets, and I thought it must be a new resort area.

I took off, trying to lope in the snow, tremendously excited. Halfway there, I plunged into a drift. My leg was miserably swollen and the cold soothed it. It felt so good that I let it seep in for a few minutes. Then I crawled out and moved on, keeping my eyes on the houses, wondering if I would have to break in, wondering if there would be provisions and warm clothes inside.

I saw him and stopped short. A man with long, light hair was standing on the deck of the highest house, stretching. He was wearing a robe. His arms were out and the white robe billowed around him.

"Hello!" I called, out of breath. "I've been in a plane crash. I need help."

He did not turn at my call. I noticed a large black cross hanging around his neck. I was confused. And then I realized that it was not a man at all, but a statue. I had seen such statues in the Alps, erected to mark the place where someone had died or been saved, or to watch over the traveler. I figured artists probably lived in those houses, with a statue like that on their deck.

Sled tracks were all over the place, crosscutting the snow, running every which way. Kids had been playing there recently. I could even hear them. The sounds of their laughter floated from beyond the houses like the ringing of clear glass bells.

It was so incredibly lovely, finding these houses nestled so

120

perfectly into the mountain. There must be a road; there had to be. I reached the first of the houses and stopped.

I stood there for a long time, rubbing my hand over the giant rock. There was no house, only the massive rocks curving into the land. I blinked. There were no houses, no statue, and no children. My hands verified it; I touched the rock and the houses vanished. I stopped to look at what I had been so certain were sled tracks in the snow and realized the trails had been made by bits of snow that had rolled down the slope, gathering more snow and momentum, leaving a cross-hatch of lines.

My mind had created all of it, had fabricated the whole thing. I had seen what I wanted to see and it had been beautiful, but it had not—been there.

I looked all around me. It was quiet, utterly quiet. I was alone. I looked back across the bowl, to the place where I had left the trail, and I understood how much the detour had cost me. I had lost time and sacrificed strength. In moving across the bowl, I had not shortened the distance I had to travel down. I sighed. There was nothing to do but get on with it.

The bottom of the snow slope was proving to be much farther than it had seemed from above. At least two hours had passed, and I had another half a mile to travel just to get to the base of the snowfield.

I moved along, thinking about the wonderfully organic houses my mind had created, how much in harmony with the land they had been. Maybe, I thought, it was a kind of joke—a cosmic joke. And was I going to have to contend with these pranks the rest of the way down the mountain? I did know one thing: Touch was the test. If I could touch it, it was there.

I could see the end of the snowfield ahead of me, about a quarter of a mile away. At the base, where the snow gave way to rock, standing with arms out and reaching toward me, was Jim. He was smiling his crooked smile, and he began to stride up the slope to meet me.

"Hey, I'm okay," I yelled to him. "I'm coming."

When he got to within shouting range, he disappeared, only to reappear a few seconds later a bit farther down the slope.

I knew he wasn't there. He couldn't have been, I was perfectly aware of it. He had no idea where I was and I understood that. I also knew how much I wanted him to know that I was okay and that I was on my way home.

12

His secretary slipped into the inner office, tiptoeing as a matter of habit on the thick carpet, trying not to interrupt the staff meeting. She passed a note to the man behind the desk, then stepped back to wait for his answer. Robert Elder glanced down at the message: *Jim Fizdale is on the phone, says urgent.* He looked at the message for a long moment, trying to think what it might mean, what was going on with Lauren.

It was 8:15 on Tuesday. Elder was holding his usual morning staff meeting in his office at Northrop Aviation, near Los Angeles International Airport. The company made fighter planes, and Elder was in charge of its flight-test program. He rose to follow his secretary out of the room. In the outer office she handed him the phone and then, because she sensed a crisis, moved away from her desk so he could sit down.

He listened for several minutes, frowning. Then he sat down abruptly.

Jim was excited but efficient. He gave details of the search he had set in motion.

"Good," Elder said twice, in his commanding-officer's voice, low and booming. He jotted down names and phone numbers, asked a few terse questions.

Jim explained that he was now at the veterinary hospital, that he planned to be there a good part of the day. He would let Elder know where to reach him if he left.

The conversation lasted for ten minutes or so. At the end Elder said, "You did exactly the right thing; you followed all the correct procedures." What he didn't say was that he would take it from there. He considered that obvious: Lauren was his daughter.

He walked back into the meeting and didn't say anything. The staff was absorbed in the discussion. He sat at his desk for ten minutes, letting it sink in. *Lauren is missing, presumed down.* Jesus! How many times had he heard that phrase in his life? At that precise moment he knew exactly what he wanted to do: He wanted, *needed,* to get in a plane and go looking for her. He had to go out there and find her.

Harry O'Connor was watching him. They had been friends for too many years for O'Connor not to know that something was wrong. But he waited. He waited until Elder motioned to him, and the two old friends left the room.

They were much alike, the two ex-Navy test pilots. Their careers had paralleled each other, first in the Navy and then at Northrop, where O'Connor worked in Elder's department. Each had a reputation for being able to fly anything that could get off the ground, and each preferred flying fighter planes to anything else.

Though Elder was larger, the two men looked somewhat

alike. Both had thick, wavy hair and tended to dress in the short-sleeved shirt and tie that had become a uniform in the Southern California aeronautical industry.

O'Connor listened as Elder explained what had happened, interrupting only to ask a few practical questions. Then the two huddled over Aeronautical Chart CG-18, which covered California and Nevada, working to reconstruct the most likely flight path between Fresno—the pilot's last point of contact—and Jackrabbit Flats in Death Valley. They drew a straight line to establish the most direct route. It crossed the mountains just north of Mt. Whitney, the highest spot, and moved on through Owens Valley, south of the town of Independence and north of Lone Pine.

O'Connor knew the whole area well. Northrop planes went back and forth to Edwards Air Force Base, and much of the testing was done in the restricted desert region that bordered the area. He also knew enough about the mountains to hope that the Cessna had made an emergency landing on the eastern side, maybe on one of the dry lake beds sprinkled between Owens and Death valleys.

What neither man said, but both understood, was that the Cessna had gone down in an isolated place. Had it landed on any small airstrip—or even in a cow pasture or on a desert road—there would have been some word by now. But there *were* a few desert stretches remote enough to account for the long silence. That was their best hope and both knew it. They also knew that the most likely place for a plane to go down was in the Sierras. And they were aware that if the Cessna had crashed in the mountains, there was little chance for anyone to survive.

"What about the pilot?" O'Connor asked.

Elder answered without looking at him. "Veterinarian, weekend pilot. Total of 213 hours, 46 in the type."

O'Connor didn't say anything. He didn't have to. Between them, he and Elder had logged more than 20,000 air hours.

125

They had flown in all kinds of conditions, and each had had a share of close calls.

"Risks have been the name of the game all my life," Elder had said once, trying to explain why he did what he did. "But they were risks I had to take and they were taken for calculated reasons."

Northrop had three planes equipped to search for downed aircraft. Elder knew they would be made available. All he had to do was ask.

"I'll go," O'Connor said. "I'm the logical one."

Elder nodded. He knew what his friend was saying, and he knew he was right. No matter how much he wanted to go, he was not the one. Not this time. Anyway, he would have to be with his wife, Irene. He couldn't leave her alone, not with this.

He decided that only one of the company's planes would join the search. "The Civil Air Patrol and the Air Force already have about a dozen planes up," Elder explained. "To many planes flying around in those mountains without a central control can be hazardous."

"Right." O'Connor agreed. "I'll take the Beechcraft Baron and head north to Fresno. That way I can pick up their trail and trace the flight path over the mountains." He pressed his thumb into a point on the map. "I'll cross here, at Kearsarge," he said. "That's the logical place to cross. Then I'll drop over to Owens Valley and go on into Furnace Creek. If no one has sighted them by then, I'll swing north to check out the small lake beds in here." He pointed again to the flight map. "Then I'll go on up to Bishop and recross the mountains, scanning south along the crest."

It was already decided that George Mehelic, a dispatcher at Northrop, would be in charge of a kind of command center. He would keep in touch with the Air Rescue Center and would keep track of all search efforts, filling in Elder whenever anything new developed. He would also contact the Inyo

County Sheriff's Department in Independence, at Elder's request, to make sure no names would be released. He didn't want any news reports out before all the relatives had been notified.

Mehelic talked to the sheriff and then buzzed Elder's line. "They know a plane is down," he reported. "The sheriff's deputy says they'll cooperate. He'll keep us posted."

"Good," Elder answered. He got up, closed the door, and dialed his home number. There was no answer and he was glad. He had simply wanted to find out if his wife was home. He would not have told her on the phone, but he thought she probably would have sensed that something was wrong. He would go to the house to wait for her, as soon as he called Craig.

His son, Craig, was twenty-six, three years younger than Lauren; he worked for Northrop as a motion-picture photographer. His job was to record what the fighter planes could do. One of Craig's stills—a spectacular blowup of a fighter on aerial maneuvers—hung on the wall behind his father's desk.

While he waited for his son to come on the line, Elder debated if he should ask him to go home too. Craig was close to his mother, and maybe he should be there. Elder decided against it just as Craig answered.

"I've got some bad news," he started. His voice broke and he tried again. "Your sister—" He couldn't go on, couldn't get the words out, couldn't seem to get steady. He could feel the confusion on the other end of the line. He tried a third time, choking out as much of an explanation as he could, trying to bring his voice under control.

Craig was stunned, by the news and by his father's loss of control. He had not thought his father could be so shaken.

"I don't want your mother to hear it from anyone else," Elder explained. "I'm worried that it might get on the radio or somebody might call the house. I'm going home, but I think you should stay at work and come by later." Elder hung up and leaned back in his chair. He blew his nose and told himself he had handled the call to Craig badly, too emotionally.

"Huh!" he said out loud, surprised at himself.

Over the years he had lost friends, and some of them had been close. Men he knew had taken off and had never come back. Some were listed as missing, and for a while there had been some hope. But they had not come back, had not been found. The war years had been brutal. The first time he lost someone he cared about he had been even younger than Craig. It had hurt. It always hurt, but never like this. Nothing had ever felt like this.

He heaved out of his chair, a big man with thick, curly hair. He was heavier than he had been in the years when the space program was getting under way, when he had been in line to go. But he had been too big, physically, in the beginning, and then it was too late. Some of the men who had served with him in the Navy—Alan Shepard and Wally Shirra—had gone. He had wanted to be part of the space program as much as he had ever wanted anything.

Until that day. That day he wanted the miracle he knew it would take to bring his daughter home alive. The trouble was that he had been around airplanes too long to let himself believe in miracles.

13

Nothing had ever looked so inviting as the ocher-colored rocks at the base of the snowfield. I was anxious to reach them, to get dry, to be warm. I wanted to get down to the warm rocks with the lizards and the living things. I was ready for something different from plunging into snowdrifts and feeling soggy, cold, and damp. The rocks looked like a wonderful change.

I managed to cover the last few feet of snow in high style. My feet flew out from under me, and I landed on my back and skidded to a stop just short of the rocks—a perfect Charlie Chaplin pratfall.

I got up, picked out a nice flat rock to sit on, peeled off my boots, and scraped out the snow. Jay's socks were soaked. The sun was warm enough to dry them but I didn't want to take the time, so I smoothed them out and pulled my boots back on. They were cold and clammy, but now that I was on dry land once more I was anxious to push on.

Pushing on, however, was altogether different on the rocks. It was not so easy. I had to watch each step, checking to make sure the rock I chose was firmly planted. Then I had to balance carefully as I hopped to the next rock. The two-inch heels that had served as pitons in the snow were a hindrance on the rocks. Twice I judged poorly and went sprawling, collecting more scratches and bruises—not enough to stop me, but enough to make me concentrate even harder on my footing.

One boot heel was slipping. The rubber cap on the heel had torn off, exposing the plastic core. The slick plastic was giving me trouble. If I could have had one wish I would have asked for the pair of hiking boots languishing in my closet at home, because now I was convinced that it was all a matter of plodding on, of persevering.

I saw that the stream bed lay at the lowest point in the canyon, where two mountain ridges came together. There was not, as I had thought, one deep, straight line that ran between the base of the two. Rather, the ridges meshed like the fingers of two clasped hands, so the stream bed made a series of sharp turns.

I picked my way around the first bend only to find another bend behind it. I turned four or five of these corners before I admitted that I had no idea how many more lay ahead. It was exasperating. The only thing I could be certain of was that if I stayed with it, taking a rest now and then, I would eventually come out of this maze. Eyes to the ground, I pressed on. The rocks taunted me. I was determined not to let them break through the calm I now felt. I knew that I had the stamina, that I would win. I knew too that it was painfully slow going, picking among the rocks, avoiding the sharp edges when I could. I told myself that the real danger was behind me, left high on the mountain, but I knew that a broken ankle could kill me too. I had to be just as vigilant, just as careful, as ever. I could not let up even for a moment.

Scrubby sagebrush and sparse pine trees were beginning to appear on the high desert terrain. As I moved down the mountain I noticed new varieties of plants and grasses, most of them spiky and harsh. I was glad I didn't have to contend with the lush vegetation of the western slope. The rocks were enough.

A kind of interior safety valve seemed to be operating. Now and then it would signal me to stop and rest, to pace myself. I would climb on a flat rock, stretch out, and let the sun warm me. I would take the time to look up and about and breathe in the perfect quiet. I felt comfortable in this wilderness. Never in my life had I been so alone, but it did not seem an alien place and I was not afraid.

My eyes scanned the rocks for small animals, but I saw none. Perhaps it was too early. Snow was piled high in the shadow of the rocks, and it was still very cold out of the sunlight. *All the more reason for you to get on with this journey down the mountain,* I told myself. I got up to move on. A nap in the sun would have to wait. I needed to get to the lower elevations where the air would be warm, in case the sky suddenly clouded over.

I rounded one bend, then another and another. Once I thought: *This is all, no more. I won't accept another bend in this blessed mountain.* But there were more bends, and I did accept them. I trudged on, fussing and annoyed. I remembered standing on the crest the day before, telling Jay that it would take me a couple of hours to hike out to the desert. *Telling Jay.* Yesterday seemed such a long time ago. Time was deceiving, distances were deceiving, everything was deceiving.

The only thing I could be certain of was that the stream bed *had* to wind its way out to the desert. I kept telling myself that it was just a matter of staying with it, of keeping

131

strong and calm. After all, I thought, it was a matter not of skill or daring, but of simple determination. "We shall overcome." "One step at a time." "Keep on truckin'." The slogans, the clichés, again flashed on and off in my mind, and I moved on, choosing my rocks with great care and a certain amount of malice.

About that time, without knowing that I was doing it, I began to look for signs that others had been there before me: a smashed Coke can, a pop top, a cigarette butt, some indication that I had moved into the realm of people. I would be sure I had spotted something, but a Neolite heel would turn out to be a flat piece of granite or a shoestring would be a shard of rotten wood. The irony was not lost on me. I wondered how many times I had been irritated to find that same kind of litter along hiking paths.

Before long I began to feel that people really *were* close by. I was sure that when I made my way around the next bend I would discover some tangible evidence. As I hopped from one rock to the next, doing my repetitive balancing act, I directed my attention almost totally to the ground. The mountains soared all around me but they were not part of my view, though now and then I would glance up to the slopes that came down to the stream bed.

The feeling swelled, filling me with such certainty that I wasn't at all surprised to come upon a small hut with broad, flat leaves thatched over a framework of branches, the kind of shelter a camper might put up. I didn't stop to examine it, since I was sure the ranch would be around the next bend.

I hurried on. Just as I had hoped, I saw a farmhand working on a hillside above me, a Mexican wearing loose white clothes and a straw hat.

"Hello," I called out to him.

He didn't turn around but kept working in the garden. Maybe he didn't understand English.

"Hola!" I tried again in Spanish. "Hablas español? Socorro! Me duelen las piernas!"

Still he did not turn around.

I knew then that he was another fiction. Like the man in the white robe, the Mexican peasant was not going to help me, was not even going to recognize my presence. I had not seen his face but I knew I was of no concern to him. It was as if *I* didn't exist. I thought to myself: *You don't, not for him.*

Yet I couldn't shake the feeling that a ranch house really was nearby. I hurried around the next bend, certain it would be there. I went around another bend and another, but there was no sign of the ranch, no sign of life at all. This arid eastern slope of the Sierra Nevada was wild and dry, as it had been for thousands of years before I came and would be for thousands after I was gone.

As I moved continually down, there were a few sandy stretches. The sand consisted of coarse granite, and there wasn't much of it, but it was easier to walk on. The slopes that came down to the stream bed were too steep to attempt. All I could do was continue the interminable rock hopping, slipping now and then on the plastic heel, cursing under my breath.

The sun was high. Sometimes I would work up a sweat struggling among the stones. Then I would scoop up a handful of the snow that lay in patches in the shade of rocks. Sometimes I would wait for it to melt in my hand, but more often I would just pop it into my mouth. Once, as I bent to scoop some up, I noticed a tiny, fragile wildflower, and for a minute I stood looking at it, trying to understand what there was about it that so moved me. It was exquisite, delicate and minute, growing in the wild. How brave it was to bloom in this harsh land! But had I not come along, no one would ever have seen the flower. The thought occupied me as I trudged on.

I was not so much tired as exasperated. The rocks kept coming at me, and there was nothing to do but meet them. I was ready for a new kind of terrain—anything but the rock-strewn path—but I had no choice. As far as I could see, the rocks continued.

She was sitting on a rock ledge just above my head, in the shade of an overhanging boulder: a middle-aged woman with a sketchbook and a tool kit fitted out with paints. She startled me because I didn't see her until she was perhaps fifteen feet away. She was sketching wildflowers and she looked the part perfectly. Everything about her was no-nonsense, from her blue denim slacks to her red-checked shirt, stout Oxfords, and white ankle socks. She was the kind of woman you would expect to find alone in the desert, sketching the flora. She probably knew everything there was to know about wildflowers, and I was sure she would be able to identify the single tiny blossom I had found in the snow. Clearly, she was absorbed in her work.

I stood on a rock, waiting for her to look at me. She was wearing a straw hat that concealed her face, but I was sure she had noticed me. It would have been hard not to, I was so close.

She did not look up. She continued sketching and I understood that she was not going to acknowledge me. I supposed she valued her solitude and considered me an intrusion, but I decided it didn't make much difference. I knew that I was going to have to walk out of this on my own, that I was the only one I could count on. So I walked away from the solid-looking lady in the white ankle socks. I left her sitting there in the shadow of the rock, sketching wildflowers. Somehow I knew that the phantoms were peripheral to my purpose, which was to get myself off the mountain and home again.

I never once thought that I might be losing my mind. Perhaps I might have been afraid, had I not at one time in my life experimented with psychedelic drugs. I knew, from that experience, the kinds of excursions the mind can take. Clearly, my mind was extraordinarily busy, superimposing patterns on the landscape. The Mexican peasant, the woman

134

artist—they were likely candidates to come reeling out of my subconscious, themes I might myself have used.

I hummed as I went along, trying not to let the bends in the stream bed get the better of me. From the moment I had lowered myself over the side of the crest early that morning I had been aware of a feeling of pure physical strength. But it was really more than that. It was strength tempered by balance, a kind of power that seemed to spring from some untapped well. It was as if I had been granted an unlimited supply of energy, and I was amazed and confounded by it. I don't know how it happened, especially after the long, dark night in the plane with Jay. I had neither slept nor eaten, yet I felt restored. Adrenalin seemed an inadequate answer for the strange feeling of power and balance—the *grace* that had come to me.

The brush was getting thicker, pulling at my skirt and scratching my legs. The sun was still high, but it was moving into the afternoon. I couldn't tell how much farther I had to go, and my patience was fraying. I turned another blind corner, bracing myself for what I was sure would be yet another bend. I did not want to let myself be disappointed. I no longer believed in magic paths that led to the desert flat; I believed only in rock, rock, and more rock—hard and tough and likely to trip me up—exasperating rocks sprinkled around an endless progression of curves.

I was not prepared for what I saw when I came around the next corner. Suddenly I was standing on the brink of a tremendous drop. I was at the top of a dry waterfall that fell away, straight down, to a canyon floor more than one hundred feet below. Sheer rock walls rose to either side of me. There was no way to go, none.

"No-o-o," I howled, shocked at the bleating anguish I heard in my own voice.

I was trapped.

I waited for a few minutes, and then I did the only thing I

could think to do. "Help!" I yelled at the top of my voice. I could hear the word ricochet down the canyon. "Please somebody, help me!"

There had to be forest rangers around—or campers or somebody. At Yosemite people crawled all over the place; you couldn't get free of them.

"Can anybody hear me?" I shouted again. "Please! Hear me!" My voice echoed away, swallowed by the silence.

I scanned the terrain below me, looking for a sign of life—a road, a path, anything. But all I could see was a wild and empty country, utterly empty. Snow lay blue and quiet in the shadow of the rocks. The sun shone and everything was heavy with silence. The only sounds were the catch of my breathing, the thumping of my heart.

No one had heard me. No one was going to help.

14

Dumb, dumb, dumb. How colossally, stupendously, magnificently dumb of me not to have figured out that this would happen. I laughed a little hysterically. Anyone with even the smallest amount of gray matter would have guessed that there would be sheer drops on the eastern edge of the Sierras. It was a vertical landscape. Why should I have assumed that the descent would be gradual? What would make me think that hopping along the rocks was all I had to do to get down off the mountain?

I was stuck for sure this time. I had done myself in for good. I figured I was more than halfway down, so there was no sense trying to go back up; and the only way down seemed impossibly blocked. I was caught in between, in a no man's land.

I supposed that as the snowfield melted it found its way to the valley by roaring over this precipice, this clean granite face of the cliff. I tried to remember the basic lessons a mountain-climbing friend had once given me. We had spent a day in Berkeley at Indian Rock, a thirty-foot chunk of stone used by the citybound to get some practical experience. I had learned a little about how to read rock and to negotiate the face of a cliff.

I knew that there was no way down, but out of curiosity I lay down on my stomach and began to study the drop. At first glance the granite had seemed smooth and slick, but on closer examination I realized that it was pitted and cracked. It had the kind of crevices that offered good fingerholds and toeholds.

The longer I inspected the granite, the more I saw. There was a series of narrow ledges at ten-to-twenty-foot intervals along the hundred feet of the fall. I gauged each to be almost the height of a freeway overpass. So the drop was broken, as nearly as I could tell, into sections. I told myself that it might just be possible if I were careful, very, very careful.

I had no choice. There was nothing to do but try to climb down. I had no place else to go, and time was running out. If I tried to spend the night here I might freeze to death.

I took off my boots, tucked the socks inside, and dropped them over. They landed on the first ledge, in a puddle of melted snow. I was going to need all my fingers and all my toes, and I was grateful for the thick callouses that my karate lessons had produced.

I moved backward over the side, feeling with my toes until they found a hold on the face of the rock. I repeated to myself what I had been taught: *Stay bunched up, keep your hands and feet close together, test with your fingers and toes for firm holds.*

Monkeylike, I began to move down the cliff. One bad choice of footing and I would fall. I could feel it, the terror of coming loose from the wall, of falling free, of breaking on the rocks below. *Oh, God, don't think about it,* I told myself.

138

Concentrate on not reaching too far, not getting all spread out.

My toes touched the first ledge and I sank down, relieved—and worried. I was in a more precarious position here than I had been above because now I was committed to negotiating the rock wall. I could never get back up, and I had managed to cover only the first dozen feet.

At the same time, I realized that something extraordinary was happening. This part of the climb had not been easy, but it was infinitely more perplexing—and exciting. I couldn't seem to make a wrong move. Something was happening between my body and the face of the dry waterfall. They seemed to understand each other.

I had known the feeling before. I had it sometimes when I was surfing. I would catch a big wave and ride it on and on, sensing that I was part of the sea. I didn't have to think or even make an effort. We just flowed together, my body responding without any command. And it happened to me at other times—the best times when I was jumping a horse. Then everything was so finely balanced that I knew I could do no wrong, that whatever move we made together was right. But I could not believe that I had this feeling on a sheer granite cliff in a mountain wilderness.

I studied each drop, then threw my boots over the side and followed them down. I concentrated, thinking only of the rock and each move. I reached for a niche with my right toe; it was there. Everything was working. It was hard, but there was a kind of rhythm to it. The one thing I knew not to do was to look up; that would undo me. I wondered if men who wash windows in skyscrapers ever look up or down.

At the next ledge a surprise was waiting for me. In this rockbound place a tree trunk had fallen out of nowhere and was lodged along the side of the gorge and the next ledge. It was a natural staircase, a perfect ladder. The branches had been stripped away, so only the spine of the tree remained. I tested to see if the wood was rotten and if the tree was firmly wedged. Discovering it was fine, I scrambled down and plopped onto a cushion of snow on the ledge. I sat there for a moment, exultant. I felt that I could relax a little now, since it was going so well. As soon as the thought came into my mind, a caution light went on. *Keep it together,* I said to myself. *A fall here could mean a broken back, or a broken leg.* I said it out loud—"Keep it together!"—and was embarrassed to hear my voice break the silence. I lay down on my stomach again and peered over the ledge to see what the next drop was like.

"Ahhh!" I couldn't help but sigh. Below me was the widest ledge of all—perhaps fifteen feet—and in the middle, in a pool of sunlight, was a hollow filled with melted snow. It looked at least three feet deep, and it was the most beautiful thing I had ever seen.

I slipped out of my clothes, bundled them together with my boots, and pushed them over the side. Then I eased myself into a wet trough on the face of the cliff and let myself slip into the water, landing with a splash.

It was cool and wonderful. I ducked under, drinking deeply. Then I bathed my wounds and tried to wash off the soot and the sweat, the blood and the grime and the pain. It was everything I had ever imagined a pool in paradise to be. I lay back and floated, feeling comforted for the first time since the crash.

After a while I pulled myself onto the smooth rocks and lay back, letting the sun warm me, closing my eyes and drowsing, emptying my mind and resting on the edge of sleep.

Someone was staring at me. I could feel it. I tried to push the feeling away, but it wouldn't go. I opened my eyes to see a man perched on the rock wall directly across from me, about fifty feet from my ledge. As soon as I looked at him he turned away, but I knew he had been staring at me, I knew it for sure. Each time I averted my gaze, I could feel his eyes return to me.

He was a perfectly ordinary-looking man, squat with dark-rimmed glasses and curly red hair. He was wearing gray trousers and a lime-green sports shirt with short sleeves. The peculiar thing about the man was his stance. He was hanging out from the cliff like a gargoyle, his arms behind him, his head and chest thrust forward.

I could not catch his glance. He was, I knew, another of the dream people, benign, remote. I did not try to call out to him. I knew he wouldn't answer.

A flash of light at the top of the cliff distracted me, and when I looked back, the man was gone. It didn't matter, because what I saw high on the southern rim of the canyon sent me reeling.

Lining the rim was a row of two-story houses, and above them I could see the sun glinting off the tops of two parked cars. *Finally,* I thought, *finally it has really happened.*

Someone, I could see, had discovered the wonderful, wild canyon and had created a retreat. Others had been there before me. I could tell by the footpaths that led directly to the houses and the lawn furniture in the yards. The pool wasn't all mine after all, I thought. Others had bathed there too.

I pulled on my clothes as quickly as I could, all the while scanning the slope I would have to climb to get to the houses, trying to judge how steep it was. Snow covered it but I could see bits of plants poking through the crust. I would be able to pull myself up by using the plants. And then home, and Jim, and warmth and rest. *Soon now,* I told myself, *soon you are going home.*

The gorge cut by the stream bed was narrow at that point, and I jumped over it. I scrambled up the slope like a mountain goat, anxious to cover the space as fast as I could, going at an angle because of the steepness. When I was within a few yards of the closest house, a blond man walked onto the porch.

Suddenly I felt embarrassed, realizing how wild I must look, how disheveled. I wondered what he would think, seeing a woman coming out of nowhere.

"May I speak to you?" I called out to him.

He looked up.

"I know I look terrible," I explained, "but you see—I've been through—I'm not crazy, believe me."

An aluminum screen door banged open and a woman walked out, her hair ruffled by the breeze. She moved gracefully, like a figure in an Ingmar Bergman film, and hung a cloth on the clothesline.

"I need your help," I called to them. I wanted to be up there with these people more than I could say. I knew I would like them, would find them fascinating. There was something so complex, so intricate, about the man and the woman on the porch.

But I could not get up there. They would not help. They weren't there. Again, my God, they weren't there. I reached down to touch the bent reed that had been transformed into lawn furniture. *How could you?* I asked myself, over and over again until it hurt. *How is it possible that you could do this to yourself again?*

I saw that the paths were there, all right, but they had been made by animals, possibly mountain sheep. I had been seduced, again, by a promise of easy salvation. I had gone off on another wild goose chase, believing it was almost over. Then I told myself that from that point on salvation would come only if I stuck to the path to the desert, no matter what. Until somebody came up to me and said, "Let me help you," I would keep to my resolve.

I now realized I had scaled a precipitous snow-covered incline, one that converged into the dry waterfall at an angle so sharp that the only way to get down was to move sideways across it, just as I had on the cliff that morning. Once more I began to work myself down the slope, spiderstepping and punching my feet through the crust. My left boot zipper split open and the leather began to flop around my ankle. I pulled off the boot and flung it ahead of me down the hill, following the path it plumbed.

I was wet and cold now, and all I wanted was to return to the big ledge and get on with it. As I was telling myself to hurry, my hand slipped, and I skidded fifteen feet on my stomach before I could grab a bush to stop myself. I was shaken; the rock gorge waited below. But I'd made it back to the ledge, and I forced myself to slow down, to rest for a while. Then I looked at the sun; I guessed it was about two o'clock. I knew I had to be out to the desert by sundown, and again I felt the need to push myself harder.

The ease and assurance with which I had climbed earlier were gone. My hands and feet, numb from the trek in the snow, could no longer find the right niches in the rock. I reached too far with my right foot and then, because of that, I could not lift the left one. I was spread-eagled on the face of the rock, unable to move, unable to think. I could feel the sweat break out on my body. I couldn't hang there many more minutes. My fingers were losing strength; my grip was failing. I had to go back, back to the ledge above. It was my only hope. I would have to risk a lunge, one mighty effort to pull myself to safety. I scrambled, hitting my foot against something sharp, but I arrived intact.

I sat there, trembling at the thought of how close I had come to falling, staring at a flap of skin that hung loose from my toe. I *had* to calm down, to rest, before I could risk another try. For a while I concentrated on rubbing my hands and feet to get the circulation going. This time I wouldn't stir before I was ready to, no matter how fast the sun was moving.

143

Slowly, painstakingly I started down the next ledge, and then there was only one to go. The last dropped from fifteen feet to the canyon floor, where there was a deep snowdrift. I worked my way down the first ten feet, took a deep breath, and flung myself backward, landing in the snowdrift.

I lay in the snow, looking up, gaping at the awesome granite wall I had just climbed down. It was as close to a miracle as I had ever come.

15

Los Angeles

The white Mustang moved south on Pacific Coast Highway, past Manhattan and Hermosa and Redondo beaches, not turning until it reached the Palos Verdes hills. Irene Elder pulled into the driveway of her home a little before one. The store had promised delivery of the new washing machine that afternoon. She had wanted to be sure to be there, so she had come directly from an art history lecture she had attended. She noticed her husband's car and wondered what had brought him home in the middle of the day. A rush trip to Washington, she guessed.

She gathered the notes she had taken at the lecture and started down the steps. The Spanish-style house was built on three levels on the side of a hill overlooking the ocean. The main entry was on the second level and the bedrooms were on the third. Through the French doors she could see her husband moving to meet her.

She saw his face and knew something had happened. "What is it?" she demanded.

"There's been a plane accident," he started.

Craig, she thought. *Craig would be flying.*

"Lauren," he went on.

She looked bewildered so he started over again, telling her what had happened, all that he knew. She did not sit down but stood very straight, holding tight to the notebook in her hands, listening intently.

When he had finished she looked at him for a time. Then she said, "No. No, I will not accept that." She said it with such vehemence that he was momentarily startled. She could see how hard it was for him, that he had been making a great effort to control his own feelings.

She tried to explain. "I believe what you are telling me. I'm not saying it didn't happen, the crash." Her voice was steady, firm, and he listened to her carefully. "It's just that I know what I know." What she knew was that her daughter was alive. She was sure of it.

Bob Elder was much less sanguine; at the same time, he respected what he tended to call his wife's "spirituality." He knew that she understood Lauren in a way that he did not.

"Is there anyone you think we should call?" he asked.

"No," she answered without hesitation, "I don't want anyone to know." Again she tried to explain. "If we talk about it to anyone, especially those closest to us, it would diminish the—" She searched for a word and finally settled on *power*. "It would diminish the power," she repeated. "I think the more positive I am, the better it will be for Lauren."

People would be sympathetic; that was natural. But sympathy was negative, she felt, and she could not let anything

146

negative intrude on the certainty that infused her. *Lauren was alive.* She must keep that uppermost in her mind.

"Have you had your lunch?" she asked.

He shrugged. He was not hungry and neither was she, but she would fix lunch anyway. It would give her something to do. She knew it was important to carry on as normally as they possibly could. It was going to be a long afternoon.

She was in the kitchen when the doorbell rang. She heard her husband answer it, heard him talking. But she did not want to see anyone or talk to anyone who was not involved in the search for her daughter. So she stood there, listening. It took a few minutes for her to realize that the men were delivering the new washing machine.

She felt relieved. *How wonderful,* she thought, *to have to deal with the everyday things of life.* All the prosaic, ordinary chores were a salvation at a time like this. She thought: *My child is lost in the wilderness and still they deliver the washing machine.*

She decided to let her husband handle the installation of the machine. He could check it out, make sure everything was as it should be.

The phone rang. It was George Mehelic at Northrop Flight Operations.

"Do you have any news for me?" she asked brightly.

"No," he said, his voice calm, "no news yet. I just need some more routine information."

After she told him what he needed to know there was a pause. Then he said, "Listen, don't worry. She's going to come walking down the road any minute now and call you."

Irene Elder was pleased with his tone, with the casual, matter-of-factness of it.

"Do you really think that?" she asked.

"I do," he answered. "I really think that."

Bob Elder was standing at the sink, washing his hands. "I

147

sent the washing machine back,'' he told her. "It had a dent in it.''

His wife smiled. "I'm glad you were here to do that. I mean, I would have sent it back too. But I'll bet they gave you a lot less trouble than they would have given me.'' Then she told him about the conversation with George Mehelic. He didn't say anything. He didn't believe that Lauren was going to come walking down the road. But he decided not to tell his wife that, not yet.

After lunch the two went to the garden on the hill below their home. He did some desultory pruning while she carefully selected and cut roses for the living room—Lauren loved flowers. She concentrated on each bud and felt close to her daughter. She could picture Lauren as a seven-year-old, her hair blonde and curly, sitting very straight on a horse. She thought about all the hours she had spent watching Lauren ride. She thought about the sack of walnuts she would take along to shell, just to have something to do while Lauren had her riding lesson. She thought about how determined that little girl had been, all those hours, all those years.

When Craig came in at 5:30 he found his parents on the lower terrace, washing windows. It was like his mother to keep busy, he thought, as he went to hug her. Then he embraced his father, more formally. It was obvious to Craig that the two were in limbo, waiting. He settled down to wait with them.

Each time the phone rang Bob Elder went into the master bedroom to answer it on the extension. Jim called to let them know that he was at the home of a friend, and he gave them the number there.

When Irene Elder went upstairs to make a light supper, she thought: *The day is passing after all. I'm making it.*

Craig joined her and she tried to explain how she had come to feel as she did. "I've decided that I can't have it both

148

ways," she told him. "Either Lauren is gone or she isn't. I've decided that she isn't, that she is alive."

When Craig was with his mother he felt calm, hopeful, light. But when he talked to his father—when he understood that he was expecting the worst and why—he felt grim and heavy.

They were sitting around the table in the family room, watching the sun drop by degrees into the Pacific, when the phone rang. It was the message Bob Elder had been expecting, and dreading.

The plane had been sighted. It had stalled into the face of a mountain south of Kearsarge Pass. No activity was seen around the wreckage.

No activity. That translated, he knew, to *no survivors.*

Craig looked at his father's face and recognized that the situation was grave. His mother was even quieter now, but he could see that she had not moved from her belief that Lauren was alive. He himself did not know; he simply did not know. But the plane had been found and his sister's fate would be resolved. Now it was only a matter of time.

"It's too late to go in tonight," Bob Elder explained. "We presume the pilot planned to go through Kearsarge Pass; that's the lowest point in that part of the Sierras. Well, he missed it. He flew south and that meant he had to go 1,000 feet higher to clear the crest. He went down in Kings Canyon National Park; the park service people will send in a team to climb to the site tomorrow."

Elder busied himself with details, taking calls and passing the information to his wife and his son.

Harry O'Connor checked in at 9:10—2110, in pilots' language—when he landed at the Northrop plant in Hawthrone.

"You know they spotted the Cessna?" Elder asked, his voice sounding suddenly very tired.

"I heard," his friend answered. "A radio report came in

while I was on the ground at Fresno, refueling.'' Then, because it was a language they both understood, O'Connor briefed him on his day's search, now and then lapsing into officialese. "I went into Furnace Creek and talked to the ranger at the lodge. Then I looked over the dry lake beds and headed north to Bishop to check in with the Civil Air Patrol. About 1540 I left Bishop, heading west into the mountains, and I picked up an ELT signal. The beacon was plenty strong, Bob, but it was sharply attenuated by the high terrain. A couple of civilian aircraft, a CAP spotter, and an Air Force C-130 came in to try to help locate the origin of the signal. We looked for a couple of hours but never found it, then finally it faded. We did find an old wreck, but we couldn't be sure if that was where the signal was coming from.''

O'Connor did not say he was sorry and Elder did not say, "Thank you for going up in my place." It did not need saying, and both knew it.

After a while Elder put a leash on the family's terrier and started out for the beach. It was deep twilight, almost dark. He was thinking that they had to make some decisions. The plane had pancaked, they said, into the mountain. Flattened. That was all. It was over; there could be no hope now. The thought was whirling around in his head as he came back into the room in the gathering dark.

"Irene," he said as gently as he could, "we've got to make some decisions now. We have to talk about it."

She looked at him, waiting.

"We have to talk about what we're going to do if—when—they find her."

She knew what he meant. She took a deep breath and thought about it. *He means what are we going to do about our daughter's body.* She was not angry with him. She thought: *Isn't it remarkable? I'm not antagonistic or bitter that he is insisting we talk about it.* She understood that he needed to do it, perhaps to prepare himself. So of course she would talk to him about it. Of course she would do it, if it would help.

At that moment she understood the strength of her own resolve. She was still so certain Lauren was alive that she could respond to her husband with the tenderness he needed.

"Lauren would want to be left there, on the mountain," she said quietly. "I would want to leave her there."

"I know," he said, anguished. "I know, but we can't. The law says you can't, you have to—" He didn't finish. He cleared his throat and started over again. "Whatever— memorial—we might have should be very simple. Because she would have wanted it that way, something simple and—"

The phone rang. It was Jim. He had heard about the plane. Elder told him they were beginning to think of arrangements. He said he hoped that whatever they decided to do would be okay with Jim.

At 10:30 Craig left to go back to his apartment in one of the beach towns to the north. His mother and father retired to their bedroom.

Irene dressed for bed, lay down, and for the first time that day felt warm tears on her face. *Don't do that,* she said to herself sternly. *No self-pity. Stop it.* And then she fell asleep.

Bob Elder stood looking at his wife's face. He saw the tears, understood the effort she had made, the energy she had spent. He saw that she had exhausted herself. He was glad that she could sleep; she would need all the rest she could get, God knew.

He opened the sliding glass door that led to the terrace and walked out. The Pacific was black now, black as far west as he could see. He looked north up the coast, at the curve of lights that marked Santa Monica Bay. Lauren had lived on the other side of that bay for a time. He had been able to stand on this terrace then and look out and know she was there.

151

She had always been so willful, so independent. Even when she was a little girl, even then he had not known— what? What he could do for her. She did not seem to need him. Not just that, more than that. Underneath, he was never really sure, and he had not been able to speak clearly to her. The words would seem to get deflected; they would miss the mark.

He looked out across Santa Monica Bay and it all came in on him. His eyes filled and the lights blurred. So much had been left unfinished between them. He pressed his head into the glass that protected the terrace from the sea winds, and he wept.

He wept because they had never finished even a single chapter; he wept because she was gone; he wept because of the awful hurt.

16

At the bottom of the dry waterfall I squinted at the sun. The highest peaks to the south cast shade into the canyon. Several hours of light were left to me, time enough to get out to the desert if—

If there were no more sheer drops, no more cliffs to climb down, and if I did not let myself get drawn off course by dream people or dream houses or dream rescues. Nobody was going to help me out. I had to remember that. I had run out of time for messing around with illusions.

I pushed my feet into the soggy boots, using the belt of my jacket to tie the left boot on. It was not going to work very well, I knew right away—but it would have to do. I needed both boots, despite the high heels, to make my way over the rocks. I searched around until I found a stick that would work as a walking staff. Then I set off once more, this time stumbling along on the wounded boot.

The song *Carry It On* came into my head; I sang it in as good an imitation of Joan Baez as I could muster.

I covered quite a distance that way, using the staff to balance myself. The energy that had sustained me throughout the day was ebbing. I felt tired and my left arm ached. Every now and then I would test it gingerly; I could feel a bone moving inside it. I continued to favor it by leaning heavily on my right arm, but after a while my right hand began to hurt. It was scraped and bleeding from clinging to thorny shrubs and granite, and from hanging on to the staff.

The terrain at eye level was dull—endless red-brown rocks—yet I couldn't afford to lift my eyes for fear of missing a step and falling. As if to break the monotony, a hallucinogenic sideshow kept me entertained: A black panther, no bigger than a large house cat and therefore not threatening, crouched on a ledge above my head, glowering at me. *Imagine that!* I thought. *Carry it on.* A lion's face was chiseled into the stone, along with any number of beautifully crafted artifacts. I no longer thought of these visions as signs of life. It no longer occurred to me to go looking for whoever may have made them. I decided the Indians had left them there; it seemed a reasonable explanation. I thought a good deal about the Indians, about how they must have explored that country once, a long time ago. So I took note and went about my way. *Carry it on.*

The sun was moving; shadows began to lengthen in the canyon. Though the air was still comfortable and the sun warm, I began to think of how wonderful it would be to sit in a car with the heater on, to feel carpeting beneath my torn toes. *Oh, God, it would feel so good.*

That was when I started to think about what to say to the first people I met. Where would I ask them to take me? I had no idea where I was. I couldn't remember the names of any of the towns in Owens Valley. Should I ask them to take me to a hospital, or should I ask them to get the police? What was the protocol, exactly, in a situation like this? I mean, who were the *proper authorities?*

The phrase stuck in my mind and bubbled there. It was important to figure out who the *proper authorities* were and what relation I was to them. It was such a complex idea I had to think hard to sort it out. I was thinking as I turned the corner and came upon the woman—a rancher's wife—gathering watercress in a stream.

Her back was to me. Beige slacks covered her broad, middle-aged hips; her thick hair was pulled back in a casual twist and caught at the nape of her neck.

She was there; she really was. She had to be. As she stooped in a place where new willows choked the stream, I called to her.

"Hello," I sang out. "Listen, I need some help." I hurried to get close. She couldn't hear me, not with all the noise. I missed my footing and fell. Lurching to my feet, feeling awkward and foolish, I struggled to cover the distance that separated us.

"Could you just wait for me?" I called, knowing she couldn't hear me yet. "I need a doctor and—"

Finally I was there. I reached out to her.

"Thank you for waiting," I said, and my voice cracked. "Oh, damn damn damn," I wailed. The rancher's wife was a five-foot block of dun-colored stone. I stifled the whine I could feel rising in me; I swallowed the disappointment coming into my throat. Then I thought of the last hours with Jay. I would not whine and I would not cry.

I had been so sure. I had even known that she was picking watercress. *How could you have known that?* I asked myself. *How?*

But the noise—there really seemed to be a noise. I had probably been so absorbed in the rancher's wife that it had not registered. It seemed to be the sound of water. I looked over toward the dry stream bed. It had suddenly filled—fed,

155

I concluded, by an underground spring. There it was, splashing along, sparkling in the sun as it tumbled clear and clean over the rocks. Or was it? Praying that it was real, I limped over to it and lay flat on my stomach. It looked so real. I extended my arm to touch it. It was real. I scooped up water and drank; I let it splash over my face. I drank long and deep; the water was sweeter than any I had ever tasted. The sound of it rushing down the mountain was comforting, and it kept me company.

In the early evening light everything seemed warm and glowing. The good, sweet water filled my stomach. I sat down on a stone and considered my boots. They were shot; from now on, I decided, I would travel in the water. The walls on either side of the canyon were too steep to offer an easy alternative path. I peeled off the boots and left them behind.

The water was no more than knee-deep. I would hop from rock to rock whenever I could, keeping my eyes out for flat, dry steppingstones. As often as not I would wade into the stream, the icy waters chilling my feet and legs.

Once I was in the world of water, the vegetation changed remarkably. Willow thickets choked the stream with new spring shoots; they were a bright maroon, the color of blood in veins. The air was full of the smell of piñon pine and sage. Ephedra bushes began to appear, along with rabbitbrush. And the grays and blues were relieved, now and then, by a bright orange-and-yellow lichen on the rocks.

Walking in the stream was novel at first, even refreshing. But after a time it lost its appeal, just like every other phase of the descent. Water travel became tedious then, another test of my patience and my endurance.

I continued to search anxiously for a shred of foam rubber, a wad of tinfoil, any bit of human clutter. Indian paintbrush would be beautiful another day. Blue monkshood and woolly parsnip and all the other kinds of desert flora could be examined on another trip. That day all I wanted to see was an old beer can or a cigarette butt.

The shadows in the canyon grew deeper. Even though the stream was still fully lit and warmed by the sun, I knew I had to hurry. But when I came upon a perfectly oval rock I could not resist pulling myself onto it, turning my water-chilled feet to the sun, and allowing myself to doze for a few minutes. I was bone-tired. I needed to rest, to give my aching body a small respite.

Then I was up again and off. I had to keep moving. People were worried about me; they were waiting and I had to let them know. Slipping, sliding, sometimes falling on a moss-slick rock and bruising my feet, I moved on.

With all the new vegetation I expected to see some reptiles. But I saw nothing, no animals at all. It was as if they had abandoned that canyon, that country. The only sounds were made by the water and my own breathing. Then, super-imposed on those sounds, another, louder sound began to grow—a roar, constant and full of fury. I knew before I reached it, before I could feel the spray on my face, that my idyllic little knee-deep stream was about to take a plunge over yet another abyss. I knew that this time the waterfall would be wet.

It was magnificent. The stream plummeted some fifty feet, throwing up an icy mist. A wall of granite rose to the right of it for a hundred feet above the fall, and high on the top of that was a fringe of pine forest.

To my left was a gradual slope that lifted above the fall. It was of sand and loose rock, with an occasional scrubby bush. I was afraid I might bring a storm of rocks down upon me if I tried to climb it. But it was a risk I would have to take; there was no other way to follow the stream. I gathered my haunches under me like a horse getting ready to jump, and I attacked the hill.

Scrambling, pulling myself along from rock to rock, bush

to bush, I moved with a determination that surprised me. It was not as hard as I had imagined. With a final burst of energy, I reached the top. From there I could see that the rest of my journey would be a gradual descent to the desert.

I sank into the sand up to my ankles and felt glad—glad that the sand was warm on my feet, glad that there would be no more surprises. I could almost count the number of bends left to negotiate—no more than six, it seemed. Behind me rose the needle-peaked spine of the High Sierra, its white snow cover shimmering against the purest lavender-blue sky. Ahead of me lay the desert. I was going to do it, by God. I was going to make it.

With that thought I bounded down the long, sandy slope, cutting obliquely across it to rejoin the stream. Waves of sand poured down the slope ahead of me. I wanted to shout, to yell, to yodel. *I'm going to do it. I'm going home, I really am.* Despite my aches and pains, I went leaping and dancing down, kicking up sprays of sand, slowing down only when I noticed two scorpions lifting their tails in anger at my intrusion. Animal life, at last.

Watch it, I said to myself. *No need to tangle with one of those little guys. Not now, not when you are so close.*

I managed to tumble the last few yards of the hill, doing a long sand skid that pulled me up short at the stream perhaps a mile below the waterfall. The northern bank had become too steep to maneuver, and the southern bank was thick with undergrowth in this lower section of the mountain. There was nothing to do but wade back into the icy waters.

The sun was about an hour above the crestline. I figured I could be no more than 1,000 feet above the valley floor. Help was just around the corner—I was sure of it.

Not even the visions which had, in turn, beguiled and enheartened and distressed me could distract me now. My mind was still producing and directing, but I was no longer a good audience. I dismissed what seemed to be a wonderfully snug cabin with a cynical "Hah!" I was not moved one bit by a hillside full of speculative recreational homes, with huge billboards advertising them. The houses themselves seemed to be false fronts, like homes on a Hollywood back lot. I certainly wasn't going to fall for that. When I noticed the path I knew that it had been put there, like everything else, to tantalize me, to seduce me, to make me wonder and hope.

A path. Not a very grand illusion compared with the ones you've been having, I said to myself. *Is your imagination wearing out?* I looked again. It *was* a path, a marked trail. I could see that it crossed the stream again up ahead. I scrambled across the stream to have a closer look.

Don't be fooled, I warned myself.

But that is *a horse flop.* There, in the middle of the trail, was a dried-out ball of horse manure. I had never seen anything so gorgeous. I kicked it with my foot. That's what it was: genuine, one-hundred-percent horse flop. Praise the Lord!

Tears flooded my eyes and ran down my cheeks; I began to cry for the first time, and I could not stop the tears. I had found a real trail. People came here—there were bootmarks—and horses came here. I was back in the world of people, honest-to-God people. I began to cry harder.

Stop that right now, I scolded. *Enough sniveling.* But I couldn't help it. I followed the trail, whimpering, trying to keep control. *It is almost okay,* I told myself, as I might tell a child. *Any minute you are going to meet a ranger. There will be a fake log cabin where they sell keychains and curios and pass out pamphlets telling people which trails to take. And you must be presentable.* I knew I would need to convince the ranger that I really did need his help. I was going to have to make him understand that I was sane. I had to keep it together for the "proper authorities."

In this way I continued along the trail, sniffling and wiping my nose with my once-elegant silk scarf. My skirt was torn and dirty and covered with dried blood, and I tried to smooth it out. I reached up to fluff my hair and was surprised to discover I was still wearing my flying cap. I would have to remember to take it off when the ranger came; it probably made me look a little weird.

It was easier walking now. The granite sand was soft to my feet, but they were raw and aching and cold. I doubted that anything would ever feel truly good to them again. I began to look for bootprints, began to treasure each one. Every sign of a human or a horse sent me soaring. It was only a matter of time now.

Soon the canyon gave way to a broader valley. I was relieved to be in an open space again, out of those narrow canyon bottoms with their severe granite walls. I emptied my mind of all thought; it was better to move automatically, not think of the steps ahead. Wildflowers began to appear quite frequently—tiny blossoms in the arid land. Finally before me on the trail was a sign. The words were carved into the redwood and I could trace them with my fingertips.

CALIFORNIA BIGHORN SHEEP ZOOLOGICAL AREA the first line announced. Then: ENTRANCE TO THIS AREA IS PROHIBITED UNLESS AUTHORIZED BY PERMIT. ENTRANCE PERMITS ARE ISSUED BY THE MT. WHITNEY DISTRICT RANGER, LONE PINE, CALIFORNIA, INYO NATIONAL FOREST.

Inyo National Forest. I didn't even know where it was. A few steps more and the trail broadened. There, wide and open, Owens Valley lay before me. It was covered with tumbleweed and desert brush. I could see clumps of trees in the distance but nothing else, no buildings or roads or signs of life. The valley looked empty, except for two cars parked near the sign that identified this place as the entrance to Shepherd's Pass—the taking-off place for an eight-mile hike to the top of the mountain.

One was a green Volkswagen, the other a white station wagon. I eyed them suspiciously. I knew my mind was perfectly capable of inventing the cars, capable even of adding such meticulous detail as the bicycle rack on the Volkswagen and the license plate frame that identified a car dealer in Redlands, California. I walked toward the cars with my hands out. I stopped, pulled my hands away, and looked at the prints they had left on the surface of the dusty green VW.

The Volkswagen was there; so was the white station wagon. I jiggled each of the door handles in turn and found that all were locked. But the cars were there. They did exist. I had reached the desert and the two cars did exist.

I sank down next to one of them to wait for its owners to return. I could see the dirt road that had brought them this far. It was a rough path, but the cars had managed to negotiate it. Now all I had to do was wait for the owners to show up and take me the rest of the way.

I was certain I would never be able to get up again. My feet were finished; they had carried me this far and I promised myself they would go no more. I had to wait until the hikers returned.

Suddenly I felt something I had not felt in more than twenty-four hours; my bowels were signaling me. I worried that I would not have time, that the hikers would come back, so I pulled myself into the bushes. When I was finished I made my way back to the cars. With my fist I scraped the dust off the side-view mirror and looked at myself.

My face was still blackened with soot, despite my bath in the mountain pool, and there was a burn scar on my cheek; but it was me, all right. I did not look so very different from what I had remembered.

I am not sure what I expected to see in the mirror. Perhaps, in the time that had passed since I last looked at my face, I had formed another image of myself. Or maybe I expected all that had happened somehow to show in my face. In my mind I was not the same; I suppose I expected the mirror to reflect the changes.

161

I looked out over the valley. The sun touched only the highest peaks on the far mountain range, and the light was fast going. The valley that lay before me looked desolate. It was cowboy country, real out-west West, the way it is supposed to be.

I took another look at the dust on the cars. It was, I realized, at least a two-day accumulation. Even the windows were coated with thick desert dust. The people who owned the cars were campers; they might not return for days. The people in the Volkswagen from Redlands were no more help than the phantoms had been.

But there was a highway out there in the middle of the valley somewhere. I didn't know how far away it was but I could see it, a two-lane blacktop that sliced down the middle of the valley. I was going to head for it. I was not going to wait, not for the rangers who weren't there or the campers who weren't there or for anybody.

I was going out to the highway to hitch myself a ride.

17

"Horror does not manifest itself in the world of reality." Antoine de Saint-Exupéry, the French aviator and writer, wrote that, and I had discovered it to be so. In all the time it had taken me to descend the mountain I had not experienced horror. One feels horror in anticipation or in retrospect; it needs a mental and a temporal distance.

I had also discovered, that spring day, that there is little that cannot be endured. Much of the time I had felt as if I'd been possessed of a special *grace*. That is all I could think to call it, *grace*. It was as if a transcendent power had been loosed in me as I made my way down that mountain. At times during the day I'd been filled with a peculiar sense of well-being, of elation. I had fallen out of the sky, had in the most primeval sense been lost in the wilderness, and it had not overwhelmed me. It had been, even, exhilarating.

I had felt neither alone nor lonely; I was neither happy nor sad; I simply *was*. I am not sure I can explain what I mean except to say that I came to understand, as had Saint-Exupéry when he was lost in the desert and near death, that horror does not exist, that the prospect of death is neither dramatic nor even alarming. That it *is*.

Still, when I reached the trailhead marking the beginning of the valley, I was relieved to think that at long last I was safe. I had seen a road—a graded road—and metal cars. I was cold but I was not going to freeze; I could survive a night in the desert if I had to. My only concern was to let Jim know. He would be sick with worry, I was sure, so I had to get a message to him. That was my plan: to get word to Jim and go to sleep.

At the bottom of the trail I had expected to find all the usual paraphernalia of a national park. I had to face the fact that I had happened onto that rare, pristine kind of park as yet unaltered by park service free enterprise. It seemed cruelly ironic.

I was going to have to make one last trek, to the highway. Surely, I thought, it could be no more than two, possibly three miles. And if I had any luck at all, somebody would come along in a pickup truck and give me a lift into town.

I hauled myself to my feet and set out, certain that at any minute I would be discovered, that it would all be over. Those expectations seemed to fuel my imagination. As I walked away from the two cars, visions again began to bombard me. Trees and rocks and bushes were transformed into bicyclists and young men in pickup trucks and Mexican farmhands. I chased them all, pleading with each one, begging them to help me, to talk to me, to recognize me.

"Please," I would call out, "I'm hurt." I struggled down one side of a fifteen-foot ravine in an attempt to get to two young men lounging near a yellow jeep on the far side. At the bottom I lost my sense of direction; for an instant I be-

164

came confused. I knew I had to get back to the road. The next time I looked, the two men and the jeep were gone.

I would vow not to leave the road again for any reason, and minutes later I would forget my vow and strike out across the desert again, once toward a whole camp full of Airstream trailers, their aluminum contours gleaming in the last light. I trudged half a mile to get to them, passing a couple my own age along the way.

"Are you people?" I demanded. "Can you hear me?"

They did not answer and the Airstream trailers disappeared, as did some elegant domed buildings and a young couple with a beautiful blond baby who were getting into a monstrously finned 1950s Plymouth. The visions multiplied like mirror images. Invariably the women looked peaceful, tranquil; invariably they were detached, neutral, unreachable. I passed junked washing machines, piles of lumber, and a scattering of infant's toys, not knowing if they were there in fact and not bothering to find out.

On the eastern edge of the valley the tips of the mountains were still catching the sun. But the valley floor, where I was, lay in the shadow of the High Sierra. I heard a droning and looked back. I could see one, then two, small planes circling at the very top of the ridge I had descended. I supposed they had spotted the wreckage, but they were up there and I was far below, where they would never be able to find me. I was a chameleon, a speck on the desert, and night was falling. I was still very much on my own.

For what must have been almost an hour I rambled around the desert, chasing phantoms, wasting energy. Then I came upon footprints. My own; they had to be. I had crossed over my own prints, which meant I had been walking in circles. I wrapped my arms around my body, too weary for anger, beyond disappointment. *This can't be happening, not now.* But it was. I was angry and irritated beyond all measure. For

165

the first time I felt stymied, frustrated. The journey had taken on a nightmarish quality. I would try to move forward but I was being pulled back. I tried to think.

Finally I realized that if I followed my footprints they would lead me back to the trailhead, back to the cars. And the sign. So I followed my own tracks and they took me to where I had been an hour before. I knew how much time I had lost, but I felt a small comfort in returning to a place I knew, with objects that could be touched. By that time the soft rosy glow of the desert sunset had evened out to a dull and flat gray.

Then, as a deep twilight fell over the valley, lights began to blink on, shining points of reference in a darkening world. I could see one long, steady strand of lights in the distance and I knew it had to be the highway. I made up my mind: Lights equal reality. I told myself that I would ignore everything but the lights.

Darkness enclosed the valley; it was a moonless, star-filled night. Even with the lights I could not trust myself to head out across the desert in a straight line that would take me to the highway. I had already found out how easy it was to lose my sense of direction. So I decided to stay with the road, trusting that eventually it would lead me to the highway.

The road, however, was no more than parallel ruts in the desert; now and then stretches of it would be washed out and I would have to watch my footing. As I walked, I could see a single strong light. I figured it might be the airstrip I thought I had sighted from the top of the mountain. Then, to the north, I made out a cluster of lights which I knew had to be a town.

I walked the road toward the lights for what must have been an hour.

Then I walked another.

I passed two Mexican women, their black rebozos flutter-

166

ing like raven's wings in the wind, their faces veiled in darkness and turned toward earth. They did not look at me, and I did not try to speak to them. Once I even heard a screen door bang the way it does when a kid runs outdoors on a summer evening.

By that time I had affected a peculiar gait, raising my hips to take some of the weight off my feet and legs, walking gingerly and as lightly as I could manage. The gravel and sand felt cool in the chill desert night. I hugged my arms around me and headed for the light. As each mile passed I was sure it would be the last, only to find another and yet another ahead of me.

Sometimes I was sure the road would lead to the single strong beacon. Other times it seemed to be going toward the town. I felt as if all that existed was me and the lights. The ground plane, the horizon, all other points of reference were gone. I was floating in unbounded space with no anchors to hold me to the world. I walked toward the lights and the lights receded.

Eventually the primitive road gave way to a more substantial dirt road. Near the junction I was sure I heard a car approaching. I hurried, pushing my aching body to move faster. I did not want to miss a ride. I heard the crunch of tires on gravel; a car was close, very close.

"Stop!" I yelled. "Stop!"

It did not even slow down.

I scrambled up the incline, prepared to see the tail lights glow red as it sped away. But I saw nothing—no tail lights, no car. Only water, a fast stream rushing over gravel, the sound of it mocking me.

But the road was there. It was more clearly delineated than the other one had been, more often used. More important, I could see that it was heading straight for the single row of blinking lights; the road would take me to the highway. I

167

refused to guess how far I had yet to go. The only measure of distance that had any meaning for me was the next step. There was, I had discovered, no good way to gauge distance in the desert night.

The sagebrush grabbed at me, and rocks gouged my feet. Every large bush took on a new dimension: A carnival of animals paraded along beside me, birds with wonderfully luminous plumage, playful house cats. The heavens were full of shooting stars and I wondered at how bright and close they seemed. But I could not look at the stars or enjoy the deep peacefulness of the valley; I could look only at my feet and the dim trail, could think only of the place where the dirt road would end and the blacktop begin.

I was sure the blacktop would be smooth and comforting to my poor feet. I dreamed of how good it would feel. I emptied my mind, refusing to pause long enough to determine if the picnic tables I saw were real, if the big town boys who sat at them drinking beer would talk to me.

I followed the road; the lights lay ahead of me. I could see that the stream of lights that marked the highway was no longer so steady. Traffic was sporadic and lights in the town were going off. That meant it was getting late. I guessed I had walked five or six miles.

Once more I began to prepare myself for the all-important first meeting with another human. I had left the plane that morning with nothing but Jay's pocket knife. At the time, it seemed that anything else would get in the way. I had taken no money, no identification. Yet those were tools of survival in civilization, and without them I felt exposed. At any minute someone might pick me up. I knew I looked wild, disheveled. I knew people would hesitate. They might not even give me a ride. My feet were bare and bloody, my skirt was ripped in the back and clotted with dried blood. I belted my jacket as neatly as I could and practiced my speech.

168

"As you may have noticed, I've been in an airplane accident."

Oh, my God, no. I couldn't say that. Who would ever believe it?

"I've been in an accident." That would do it. Not a plane crash, just an accident. Then I would say, "Will you take me to—?"

Where? I realized I still hadn't decided where I would ask people to drop me off. I was convinced they would not pick me up unless I could tell them where I wanted to go. So where? I concentrated as hard as I could but the answer eluded me.

A telephone—that was it. I could call collect. Then Jim could drive down to get me.

Though I knew it would be futile, I searched through my coat pockets to see if just possibly I might have overlooked a dime. There was none. Calling collect from a pay phone was out of the question. Unless, unless I asked the driver of the car to drop me at an all-night coffee shop. A diner, that was it!

I plotted out the scene as I would play it: I would watch through the window until the waitress turned her back and then I'd hurry in so she couldn't get a good look at my bare feet and torn skirt. I would smile and speak politely—that was important; politeness was important. Maybe she would let me have a cup of tea if I promised that Jim would pay for it when he came to get me. Maybe she would even lend me a dime to call him.

Jim would come to get me if he could get time off from work. Work. Jim worked for Jay. Jay was dead. I had forgotten that Jay was dead on the mountain. And that changed everything.

I tried to think about Jay and about Jim and about what it changed, but I couldn't. I could think only about the next step. I had to concentrate on the next step.

169

If the waitress wouldn't let me stay in the diner, maybe she would direct me to the YMCA or a fire station or someplace where I could lie down and rest for a while. Except, would they let me stay if I couldn't prove who I was? Would anybody believe such a strange story? *Accident.* I would have to remember to be vague, remember not to say "airplane" accident so they might think it was a car crash. That would make better sense. People walked away from car accidents.

The questions made my mind spin. I trudged along, thinking of nothing. Then I attacked the problem from a different angle. If I could get on a Greyhound bus, perhaps they would let me pay at the Oakland terminal. I could send myself COD. I wondered if the driver would make an exception just this once, if the Greyhound Company would grant me a special dispensation. Of course they wouldn't, I told myself. I was not being very practical. "Rules are rules. Sorry, Miss," the driver would say. Then he would close the doors in my face and they would hiss at me.

Suddenly the road veered north, away from the line of moving lights. I saw that it was heading straight for town, that it wasn't going to intersect with the blacktop after all. I moaned, realizing that I was going to have to walk all the way, because the only cars out there were on the highway.

I do not know how many more miles I covered before I came to the barbed wire. Struggling through, snagging my jacket, I could hear the cars on the blacktop. The sound was fast and slick.

My road had met the highway after all, at the southern end of town. I had arrived at last. I was at the edge of a country town that was sleeping in the deep of night. It was as silent as the desert had been; no one was about.

My feet touched the blacktop, but it was not smooth. The flap of skin still hung from one toe, and I could feel each tiny pebble that embedded itself under it and in the raw soles of my feet. But I ignored the pain, ignored my body, and concentrated on the Sunland Gas sign. The station was dark; plastic banners fluttered in the wind. Not far away a glowing sign said NO VACANCY. I headed toward it. A prim, white motor lodge was set back from the road, behind a well-kept lawn.

Of course, I thought, a motor lodge was just what I needed. There would be a bed and I could get some rest. Through the window I could see a television screen flickering and a young man locked in place before it.

I rang the bell. Then I watched as he moved toward the door.

Do it right, I told myself.

He looked at me but he did not speak.

"I've been in an accident, a plane crash," I told him, forgetting that I had decided not to say plane crash. "I've walked a very great distance and I'm tired." My tone was calm; I was not hysterical. "Do you have someplace I could rest?" I finished, pleased that I had been so restrained, so rational.

The young man examined me, my bare feet and my clothes. I could feel him move away, although in fact he stayed where he was. He saw the dirt, the bloody legs. I shuffled, trying to hide my bare feet, suddenly feeling very self-conscious under his scrutiny.

"Sorry," he said finally. "Like the sign says, we're full."

I must have stared at him for a long time because after a while he added, as if it was all he had to say on the subject, "I can't help you."

He had spoken to me. He was not a phantom person, I knew that. He was sitting in the office of a motel, watching television, but he was not going to help me. I told myself I should not be surprised; all the way down the mountain people had been turning away from me. I had had lots of practice

171

in being ignored. People did not like to get involved. This young man did not want to have to deal with me, that was all. He wanted to get back to his television program.

But I needed a motel room. It seemed the perfect solution, the only possible answer, the one thing to focus on. As the young man made a motion to close the door, I quickly asked, "Is there another motel in town?"

He pointed down the highway. "At the other end of town, one block past the flashing yellow light on your right."

The flashing light on my right. I repeated the directions under my breath, wanting not to lose them, not to forget. I heard the door close and walked back to the highway, where I turned right and then right again, as I thought he had directed.

I peered at the houses. They were tiny frame buildings in need of paint, but surrounding them were big yards and huge leafy trees, poplars and oak. It was a small town, huddled on the highway, an old town left over from another time.

Before long I realized that I had wandered away from the main street, that I must have taken one right turn too many. A motel would have to be on the highway. I wobbled along, my feet tortured by the gravel and broken glass along the roadside. I walked high on my hips, trying to relieve myself of some of the pain.

Twice a car drove past me, but the driver did not stop. Slowly, painfully, I retraced my steps. Now every movement was a major commitment. I was going on because I did not want to spend the night on somebody's lawn, not when I was so close. I was moving because all I could think of was a bathtub filled with warm water and Epsom salts.

VOLUNTEER FIRE DEPARTMENT was written over the door of a new-looking building. I knocked; no one was about. I would have to go back to the highway, to find that other motel.

172

A pickup truck was parked on the main street. I walked over to it and leaned in. "I really do need some help," I said to the driver. "I don't think I can walk anymore and—"

I could have sworn someone had been sitting in the driver's seat, but it was empty. I was standing there, talking to a steering wheel. *Good grief,* I said to myself, feeling absurd. I hoped no one had seen me.

There was a grassy lawn in front of a big building marked INYO COUNTY COURTHOUSE. I wanted more than anything to sink down on it, but I knew that if I did, I wouldn't be able to get up again. I leaned on a marker instead. The inscription read DEDICATED TO THE PIONEERS OF INYO COUNTY. "MY LAND IS BEFORE THEE: DWELL WHERE IT PLEASETH THEE." GENESIS 20:15.

Dwell where it pleaseth thee, I thought. *If only I could.* The pioneers, at least, had not had to contend with motels and means of identification and pay phones. Nor, I hoped, did they have to face the cruel social dogma we call noninvolvement.

Across the street from the county courthouse was an old-fashioned hotel. The sign said WINNEDUMAH, and the porch was lined with worn rattan armchairs. It was a dusty old place, its windows draped in cretonne. There would be a lobby, I thought, and maybe people who would stare at me. And the bath would be down the hall from my room, not private.

I decided that the other motel would be better for me. But when I pushed off from the historical marker, I realized I was no longer very steady; I seemed to be weaving. Still, it was only half a block away, and I felt I could make it.

The sign on the motel said RAY'S DEN—VACANCY. I rang the bell, and an older man came out of the back room slowly, pulling himself away from a television show. He opened the door and looked at me, but he did not move to let me into the

173

little office. He was wary. One look at me and he was wary.

"I'm sorry to disturb you," I began, wanting to convince him that I was reliable and trustworthy and sane. But then the words tumbled out every which way. I told him about the plane crash and the walking and the fact that I was ever so sorry I hadn't any money, but that if he would only trust me, if he could just lend me a dime to make a phone call.

He did not seem to hear me; I started to repeat my story, when he interrupted. "I'm sorry, Miss," he said politely. "I have only one room left and it's reserved for a newlywed couple. I know it's pretty late, but I have to hold it for them. I promised."

Newlyweds! He didn't believe me. I couldn't make anyone believe me. I looked at the man. *He's afraid,* I thought.

Then he said to me, "There's a Baptist minister across the street there. He has a trailer and sometimes he lets people stay there for free. Maybe he'll even give you a bite to eat."

Numb, too tired to think, I limped away. I touched my hand to my head. The cap was still there but I hadn't the strength to take it off. I was so cold from the night chill I could hardly feel my feet. I was in the middle of a town with people sleeping in the houses all about me, but they were closed to me. It was as if I didn't exist.

This is going on too long, I said to myself, *and I don't know how to end it.*

I looked at the minister's house but it was dark, and I didn't want to go banging on doors, waking people up. It was hard enough talking to those who were awake.

All I wanted was a bath—a warm bath with some Epsom salts—and a rest. *You must not cry,* I told myself. The Winnedumah Hotel was my last chance. Painfully, slowly, I retraced my steps along the gravel path that led to the hotel. I hobbled up each step, lifting one foot and then the other, until I had climbed them all.

The lobby was paneled in dark wood, and the place smelled musty. I could make out the forms of several old sofas scattered about and a grand piano. Everything gave me the feeling that I had stepped into another era. Then I saw an old couple watching television in the far corner; I managed to cross the room before they saw me. The old man glanced up, noticed me, and moved behind the heavy oak desk, taking his position as night clerk.

He listened without understanding as I tried to explain that I was terrible weary and needed a room with a bath. I could tell by his expression that he was confused. He looked as if he wanted to ask some questions but wasn't able to formulate them. Instead, he reached behind him for a room key.

Now, I thought to myself, dreading what had to come next. *Now it's time to tell him you have no money.*

"The thing is," I began, and realized it was a bad start. I tried again. "I wonder if I could borrow a dime." *No. That's not right either.*

The old man looked even more bewildered, but he did not back away.

"The thing is, I have to make a collect phone call."

The old woman was still sitting in the corner, and she turned to look at me.

Then the door burst open and a man with a gun strapped to his hip strode in.

"That's her, deputy," a man behind him said. "That's the one."

Suddenly the old lobby was full of noise and movement. It took me a minute to recognize the older man from the motel, standing a few steps behind the officer.

"She says she's been in an airplane crash," he said. The night clerk of the Winnedumah, my key still in his hand, stood staring at me.

"Is your name Elder?" the deputy sheriff asked.

175

I nodded.

"Well, now, we've been looking for you," he said. And then, in the kindliest tone imaginable, he said the words I had been waiting all day to hear.

"Let me help you, dear."

18

I do not remember hearing the scream of the siren. I did not notice any flashes from the red light on the police car. I do remember that Sergeant Bill Gaulin of the Inyo County Sheriff's Department helped me into the front seat of the car, which was parked in front of the Winnedumah Hotel in the town of Independence. He was very gentle, very protective, and very much in control. That nice, balding middle-aged man was better than all the lumberjack rescuers rolled together. He was there and he was helping me.

The car radio crackled, and now and then Sergeant Gaulin spoke into a microphone as he drove, very fast, down Highway 395, through the empty countryside.

"Could you please turn on the heater?" I asked.

He answered, "Sure I can, sure thing."

By the time we reached the small hospital in Lone Pine, some thirteen miles away, my feet were bristling with pain.

When we pulled into the emergency entrance I tried to walk but I couldn't. My body, at last, had said, "Enough." A nurse arrived with a wheelchair and the sergeant helped me into it.

While we waited for the town's doctor to arrive, I was peppered with questions. I had to try to make them call Jim right away, had to make them realize how urgent it was. Finally I said, "Please, would you call my"—I hesitated—"my husband. I want him to know I'm okay."

"But you said it was 'Miss,'" the hospital clerk reminded me. I recanted; and after a few minutes of searching my mind for some label that would convince them of Jim's importance, I finally said "companion."

"I'm going to call your folks now," the sheriff's deputy said, his broad face all smiles. "Your father's friend has been in touch with us all day."

"My parents?" I asked, incredulous. "They know?"

I was exasperated with Jim for having made such a commotion. I had been so sure he wouldn't trouble my parents, wouldn't worry them. Suddenly everything seemed so out of control. The whole thing had grown out of proportion and I didn't understand why.

Words whirled about me and I could not absorb them all. "She was in a kind of stupor," I heard Sergeant Gaulin say, and a nurse answered, "Well, of course, she's shocked from her injuries. She's watched two people die and she's been through some pretty rough country. God knows how she did it."

A doctor appeared, a pleasant man who did not seem at all out of sorts at having been rousted out of bed in the middle of the night. He sewed up the gash in my leg, taking long and loose stitches, so that when he was finished the wound had a Frankensteinian quality to it. Then he painstakingly cleaned my feet. They were, he said, mildly frostbitten. The granite valley sand and the rocks had buffed away most of the skin

178

on the soles; they were a lurid magenta color, embedded with dirt and gravel. Sergeant Gaulin would later say to me, ''The skin on your feet was hanging loose; it looked like shredded mozzarella cheese.''

My left arm was swollen and ugly. I later learned that the radius bone was fractured. Some weeks later, when I returned to Oakland, I would go into surgery to have the bone rebroken and set with a metal plate. And several of my teeth would require capping. I looked bruised and swollen, as if I had been thoroughly beaten up. Even so, everybody kept saying that I was in astonishingly good condition, considering.

The doctor gave me something to ease the pain and a sedative to help me rest; then I was wheeled past the desk on the way to one of the hospital rooms. Sergeant Gaulin called out to see if I felt up to speaking to my mother, who was on the phone.

''Hi, Mom,'' I said, trying to sound the way I always do. I could feel her elation. She was laughing, I think, and crying too. I don't remember what we said to each other and I doubt that she does either. She promised to call Jim right away, and with that off my mind I surrendered—thirty-six sleepless hours after having left Oakland en route to Death Valley—to the cool white sheets and a deep and dreamless sleep.

Early the next morning my father took off in one of his company's small planes, heading over the mountains toward Lone Pine, with Harry O'Connor ''riding shotgun,'' as they would put it.

My father bounded into my hospital room, stopped, and stared. He looked straight at me and I looked back; then we smiled. For the first time in as long as we had known each other, there was nothing separating us—no debris, only clear space. Every word went to the heart, with an ease I could not believe. We talked and talked, fast and easy, but the thing that we both understood, after all that long time, did not need to be said. That morning we knew.

179

After a time Harry O'Connor came in and visited for a little while. Months later I would learn how he had gone up to search for me. That morning neither he nor my father thought to mention it.

The doctor had said I was in good enough condition to go home. I could fly back to Los Angeles with my father and Harry. Jim, I learned, was already on his way to Los Angeles to meet me there, at my parents' home. I realized that it had not occurred to my dad that I would be apprehensive about flying.

In any case, I was not ready to leave the hospital at Lone Pine, not that day. I needed to stay there a while longer, needed to rest between the sheets in the country hospital that sat on the edge of town. After a few phone calls back and forth, it was decided that my mother and Jim would drive up the following day and wait until I felt well enough to manage the car trip to Los Angeles.

While my father and I talked in my hospital room an Air Force helicopter was trying to land near the crest of Mt. Bradley, near the broken Cessna, to recover the bodies. The winds were too high and the terrain too steep for it to put down. At noon a park service helicopter delivered two rangers to the Center Basin, a bowl in the mountains below the crash site, and a few minutes later an Air Force helicopter landed nearby with a rescue team from China Lake. As the four started climbing toward the wreckage, one of them—a paramedic—had to turn back, so steep was the climb.

They found Jean's body 120 feet from the plane. Jay was where I had left him, his hair still dusted with snow. At first, when I talked about the snowstorm that hit us at daybreak, the weather service people had been baffled. They said there had been no snow in the Sierras either during the night or early the next morning. Finally someone suggested that the "storm" I described was actually snow whipped off the adjoining slopes by high winds. That would explain why it had

180

seemed to be coming from all directions and why, now and then, I could see patches of blue through the swirling white.

It took three hours for the rescue team to put the two bodies in slings, attach the slings to a hovering helicopter, and remove them to the other helicopter in the Center Basin. The park service rangers also removed the Cessna's electronic location transmitter—the beacon we had been counting on to lead the rescuers to the site of the crash—and brought it down for testing. The ELT had never been activated; its batteries were dead and the connections too corroded to make electrical contact.

As word of what had happened to me spread in Owens Valley, townspeople began to visit. They were kind and genuinely sorry that it had taken me so long to get help. The man who managed Ray's Den Motel said to me, "I just can't tell you how bad I felt for days after that." He said that he thought I was "on dope," and that someone had beaten me up and might even be waiting outside. "I knew you needed help," he told me. "I said to myself: *This girl's in trouble.*" That was when he called the sheriff's department; Sergeant Gaulin was, after all, nearby. I had passed the jail on my way to the courthouse. Had I but noticed, I could have walked into county sheriff's headquarters.

Sergeant Gaulin understood the townspeople's fears. "You did look kind of peculiar in that long skirt and funny hat, and you were barefoot and all," he said. I was told that the people of Independence had another reason to be wary of young strangers, especially women who looked "kind of peculiar." Charles Manson had been arrested in Inyo County and had been brought to the jail in tiny Independence, where he was held for two weeks before going to Los Angeles to stand trial for the Tate–La Bianca murders. Those Manson women who had not been arrested with him hung around the jail; and as the grisly details of the murders began to filter out, the townspeople became more and more disturbed by their presence. Then came all the newspeople and big-city lawyers, all of whom added to the town's distress. For the people of Owens Valley, the world is made up of insiders and outsiders, and all outsiders are to some degree suspect.

Yet I had managed to gain a certain acceptance because, as one of the nurses explained to me, "You were able to get yourself out of trouble. Folks around here are tired of always having to bail city people out of those mountains."

When all the figures were tallied, it was determined that I had climbed from 12,360 feet down to 4,000 feet, a distance estimated to be at least ten miles, counting all the switchbacks and side trips I had made chasing phantoms. Then I had walked another ten miles across the desert, into Independence. In all, I had covered twenty miles that spring day, half of it in what is described in one guidebook as "some of the most rugged country in the High Sierra." Shepherd's Pass is labeled a "very strenuous hike" for experienced hikers. An experienced hiker, it is said, can cover an average of fifteen miles a day on a clear trail.

By my second day in the hospital at Lone Pine I had received a lot of attention from the press. I could not understand why reporters seemed so interested in my journey down the mountain. I had done what I had to do, and it did not seem such a remarkable feat.

Late in the afternoon the nurse came in with a broad smile on her face. "Look who's here," she said. Right behind her was my mother, making small chirping sounds. She moved quickly to my bed, taking my face in both her hands, kissing me gently. *Holding back,* I thought. When she first came into the room I had felt her need to grasp me and hug me hard, but she had checked that rush of feeling and instead had held my face in her hands. She touched a bruise on my face, then quickly pulled away, making way for Jim.

He did not move toward me at once. He stood in the doorway looking at me, and I thought: *The moment isn't big enough. We have been through so much these past days, and now he is in my hospital room in Lone Pine and it isn't enough.* Awkwardly, he walked over to my bed and bent to kiss me. Then we began to talk, about the most inconsequential things.

He showed me clothes he had brought for me, explaining that he had packed in a rush, apologizing that they were rumpled, apologizing because he didn't know just what I would want. Little by little, we moved closer to the subject. My mother had brought the Los Angeles *Times* with her, and she and Jim took turns telling me how they had stood at a newsrack in a little town along the way, searching like mad through the back pages of the paper for the story and all but missing it because they had neglected to look at the front page. It was a headline story, with a picture of me, propped in my hospital bed. WOMAN'S ORDEAL IN SIERRA the banner said, and under that: REFUSES TO DIE, TRUDGES TO SAFETY AFTER AIR CRASH. *Strange,* I thought, *to see it reduced to that.*

Mother pulled her chair close to the bed, perched on the edge, while Jim sat back a bit. They peeked at my purple-and-red mottled legs and my bandaged feet and weird stitches. They oohed and ouched with me. After a while, we had a fine time going over the events of the last few days, jumbling them together in no sequence at all, each of us wanting to know everything the other knew, all at once.

Then Jim went out to find a place to stay until I was ready to leave the hospital, and my mother held my hand and looked at me. She told me then, very simply, that she had known I would survive. I did not tell her, in return, about the time on the mountain when I had thought of her and decided I would live. I could not think of that time yet.

Jim came back, and it was my mother's turn to find an errand to do so that we could be alone. He told me how our friends had gathered to wait with him through the long day and night. Then, when the word came that the plane had been found and there were no survivors, they had held a kind of memorial service, reading aloud from the Psalms.

Finally Jim and I talked, as I knew we must, about Jay. I told him that I understood how deeply divided he must feel, having lost a friend he cared about.

It was harder for me, later, to talk about Jay to his friends and family. They wanted to know how it had been, wanted me to describe the last hours. When I told them, as honestly and as objectively as I could, they would shake their heads and say it didn't make sense, that it didn't sound like Jay at all. It was only after we saw the autopsy report that we understood Jay's apathy, his inability to help himself. According to the county coroner, the cause of death was hypothermia and hemoperitoneum. A massive amount of blood was found in his abdominal cavity. He had been bleeding internally, and the hemorrhaging would have contributed to the hypothermia.

Hypothermia, or exposure, occurs when the body heat is lost faster than it can be produced. The body temperature begins to fall, and it can, and often does, result in death. People who hike in the mountains recognize the symptoms at once. Had I but known it, Jay's symptoms were classic: confusion, disorientation, behavior that is, as the doctors say, ''inappropriate.'' One of the most common forms of inappropriate behavior is an unwillingness to help oneself. A person suffering from hypothermia will shrug off all entreaties and ask to be left alone to curl up and go to sleep.

When Jay and I were on the mountain together, it had not seemed to me that he was any more hurt than I. I know now that he was. As blood filled his abdominal cavity, his pain had increased. The pressure, I am told, would have been terrible. Given the extent of his injuries, it seems to me clear that he bore his pain very well indeed. The physician who did

184

the autopsy said that, had we not crashed in such an inaccessible place, Jay might well have survived his injuries.

Jean Noller would not have, it seems almost certain. According to the autopsy report, she died of craniocerebral trauma and hypothermia. Her head injuries were so severe that brain damage was extensive.

For perhaps ten days following the accident and my descent from the mountain, Jean and Jay would appear at the foot of my bed at night, standing side by side in a rather formal pose. They were devoid of emotion, mute; they did not try to speak to me. I looked at them and prayed softly.

During that time I spent whole days sitting in the sun, trying to sort out all that had happened, trying to understand it. Friends brought me books; strangers shared experiences and, quite often, confidences. Visions are not uncommon, I have learned. It is simply that those who have them are wary about admitting it. A second-grade teacher who has hiked most of the trails in the High Sierra, including Shepherd's Pass, told me that when she is alone in deep mountain wilderness for some hours she begins to hear music, beautiful symphonic music. "Yes!" she exclaimed, "I do," as if she were as surprised by it as she imagined I would be.

Then she told of being caught in a sudden snowstorm in the mountains of New England. As she grew tired and became more anxious, she began to see all kinds of rescue at hand—cabins, men with pack animals—none of which her hiking companion saw.

And I have read about the "sounds of silence," the name old-timers in the mountains give to the unshakable feeling that someone, or something, is there, just beyond the light of the campfire.

Even my father, that usually practical man, would tell me how in the early days of jet flight, when systems were not as sophisticated as they now were, men were known to have re-

185

ported seeing things that no one else could see. And he would say to me, "I think that the apparitions you saw while coming down the mountain were more normal than not."

In his book *Memories, Dreams, and Reflections,* the famous psychoanalyst C. G. Jung wrote about the "deliriums and visions" he experienced in the days following a heart attack, days when he hovered between life and death. "I had reached the outermost limit," he wrote, "and do not know whether I was in a dream or an ecstasy. At any rate, extremely strange things began to happen to me." He felt as if he were high in space, looking down on earth from a great distance, or as if he were in a mythical garden. The visions came to him for three weeks and were, he wrote, "the most tremendous things I have ever experienced." "It was not a product of imagination," he insisted. "The visions and experiences were utterly real."

I have since returned to the High Sierra. I made the trip in August, three months after the accident. My arm was in a cast and my foot had not yet healed, but I had to go back. I felt ambivalent about the mountain; it had some power that I didn't understand. I needed to return, to see for myself what it looked like from another perspective. I had been wrenched away from it too quickly, so that I hadn't been able to absorb what it was.

Jim could not go and he did not want me to go. None of my friends could get away. Finally a woman I knew agreed to go with me.

We packed sleeping bags and all the gear we would need in my Karmann Ghia and drove south. As we began to work our way into the mountains, I could feel the anxiety rising within me, but still I went. We hiked into the Center Basin, below the place where the plane had fallen, and I was sick with fear, with anxiety, with the absolute knowledge that I should not be alive, should not have come through that experience alive. I knew then that it was time to get off the mountain, to go home. If, like a cat, I should have nine lives, I had used up eight. I insisted we hike out as fast as we could.

Another time, months later, I went hiking with a group in the Rockies. For ten days we covered the high country; then it began to rain. Feeling wet and miserable, I decided to leave my friends and seek shelter on my own. I made my way to a road in Glacier Park, where I hitched a ride that took me to East Glacier Lodge.

It was remarkable, the lodge. Built in another era by railroad barons, the structure was designed like a Swiss chalet, but on a massive Western scale. When I saw it, the only thing I could think was: *I've been here before.*

Suddenly I knew. This was the same chalet I had seen as I made my way down the mountain in the Sierras, the one that had appeared before I reached the end of the snowfield. A man in white robes had spread his arms, and I had called to him.

I stayed in the lodge for two days. It was quiet there, and peaceful. I walked along the paths of the flower garden that stretched in front of the chalet. The garden was planted with long, exquisite rows of tall delphiniums, bordered by marigolds and bright blue lobelia, petunias, and asters. I felt warm and safe, as I had known I would feel in the chalet— the haven—that had not been there.

On the second day a tremendous lightning storm sent great flashes through the sky, followed closely by slow, rolling thunder that seemed to echo through my body. Then the storm was over. The air was clear and smelled fresh, and the earth seemed to glow in the charged light. All the people staying in the lodge moved to the front, pulled there by something. Someone said, "Look!"

At the end of the garden, arching over the delphinium and marigolds and lobelia, reaching in a perfect arc, was a great double rainbow.

Standing perfectly still, I stared at it for a long time. And I more nearly understood what I had meant that morning, in the spring of my twenty-ninth year, when I scribbled on a notepad: *I want to make a bold gesture with my life.*